Picture a perfect June morning: I return from the school bus with armfuls of elderflower blossoms, intent on making cordial. With my own special alchemy this day will be captured in bottles to sustain us through the long winter months. The kitchen door is open; I carry a heavy bowl in the direction of the pantry at the precise moment the cat chooses to run in with a tiny rabbit in its mouth. I shout at him as he dashes past, then I trip, and two gallons of my sugary elixir is splashed literally and literally everywhere, including over Puss. He immediately drops his prey and dashes off, shaking mess everywhere. The baby bunny charges, bewildered, behind a cupboard. Now even I am forced to apply a little domesticity to this pandemonium. But not before I recover the sugared bunny and find a cosy box for it (to die in, I think cynically). Then at last I locate the mop and bucket, there is, to my delight, a small songbird nesting in it; and she's sitting! I can't possibly move her. Instead I find my bird book to try and identify exactly what she might be.

Life with the Lid Off

Nicola Hodgkinson

An Orion paperback

First published in Great Britain in 2010
by Orion
This paperback edition published in 2011
by Orion Books Ltd,
Orion House, 5 Upper St Martin's Lane,
London WC2H 9EA

An Hachette UK company

1 3 5 7 9 10 8 6 4 2

A CIP catalogue record for this book is available
from the British Library.

ISBN 978-1-4091-2002-5

Printed and bound in Great Britain by
Clays Ltd, St Ives plc

The Orion Publishing Group's policy is to use papers that
are natural, renewable and recyclable products and
made from wood grown in sustainable forests. The logging
and manufacturing processes are expected to conform to
the environmental regulations of the country of origin.

www.orionbooks.co.uk

For Kate and Ruby

Contents

Part One New Beginnings

1	Follow Your Dreams	3
2	Scene Setting	9
3	What Doesn't Kill Me	12
4	An Englishman's Home	16
5	Mother	22
6	Thou Shalt Not Steal	27
7	Never Explain	33
8	Pets and Neighbours	39
9	Newcomers	44
10	Our First Christmas	51

Part Two Lifting the Lid

11	Siblings	59
12	Schools	66
13	Salad Days	76
14	Star Wars	81
15	Cycling	86
16	Settling In	91
17	Home Sweet Home	96
18	Old Friends	100
19	Gentle Joys	105
20	The Picnic	114
21	Dull Women	120
22	Apples	125
23	High Tides	131

24	Village Scenes	137
25	Flourishing	144
26	The Interest Table	150
27	Toads	155
28	A Square Peg	160
29	Quails	165
30	A Lesson	170
31	Fowlplay	175
32	Cottage Teas	179
33	Binding	187
34	Limbering Up	192
35	Don't Believe All You Read	196
36	Winds of Change	199
37	Pill Popping	204
38	A Bad Habit	208
39	Blind Date	212
40	Easter	217

Part Three Autumn

41	A Celebration	225
42	A Family Christmas	228
43	Let Them Eat Cake	232
44	Empty Nest Syndrome	235
45	God's a Bugger	241
46	Apologies to a Water Hen	247
47	The Decline	250
48	Compass Points	254
49	Another Milestone	257
50	The Fall	262
51	Harvest Time	266
52	Osmosis	272
53	Moving On	275
	Acknowledgements	279

Part One

New Beginnings

Chapter 1

Follow Your Dreams

I sprint up the hill, but not fast enough to catch my horse, which has just broken into a canter. Doris is harnessed to a gypsy wagon containing the full complement of my children. Joe, the April baby, waves to me from the back window gloriously unaware of the impending crisis. I can't see Elfie and Dan, but I imagine they're rattling about like peas in a pod. As I run, I weave about the road to avoid the avalanche of pans and kettles that have dislodged themselves from beneath the jolting wagon . . .

Faced with a steep hill, a good wagon horse will automatically change pace in order to reach the top without losing momentum. This is fine as long as you are prepared; but as I dingle along at her head delighting in other matters, Doris catches sight of the incline before I do. Off she goes with my children as I look on aghast. The wagon rocks and rolls behind her, while pots and pans jump off their hooks and tumble back down the road. Now, I deliberate, do I catch the horse, implicit in which would be rescuing my children, or try to

3

grab the utensils while ignoring the ire of passing motorists? Maternal instinct triumphs over worldly possessions, vital as they are, and I take off after the horse.

At the brow of the hill the most extraordinary thing happens: Doris, worth every penny of the small fortune I paid for her, comes to an abrupt halt, hangs her head and takes long, deep breaths. When I catch up, Joe is clapping his hands and chanting, 'More, more!'

The children think the whole thing is a complete gas and are laughing their heads off. Until, that is, I send them back down the hill to gather everything up.

Let me start at the beginning. Beside my bed hangs a small embroidered picture; on it is sewn a sun, a star, a puffy white cloud and a rainbow. Written across the centre is *Follow your dreams*. It's the first thing I see when I open my eyes in the morning and I love it.

I suppose we all have dreams, but not everyone is lucky enough to realise them. As dreams go, mine was modest: to own a wagon, a brightly painted gypsy wagon. Like Toad of Toad Hall, from the first moment I glimpsed a bow top, I knew I must have one. With a horse, my children and a love of the countryside, I would wander the lanes of this green and pleasant land, make clothes pegs out of hazel wood, glean food from the hedgerows and generally get up motorists' noses.

The latter I became aware of only after a while. Instead of the cheery waves and smiles I naively imagined, far more frequently our lot would be a gesturing of fists with the occasional addition of blasphemy.

We have been invited to a local steam fair for the weekend, to 'add a little interest', I think were the words of the chap who asked us. I am in my element as I pack the wagon with all our needs, the children and two bantams. Then I harness Doris to this charabanc and set off on our adventure. On the whole, modern roads are not conducive to a horse-drawn wagon meandering along at around three miles per hour. Gone, sadly, are the halcyon days of Toady wending his way along sun-filled country lanes. Instead there are empty grain trailers rattling or overly full ones on a mission to get crops home before the rain.

After a journey of about fifteen miles we arrive exhausted. With only three hours of daylight left, there is much to be done before we can even start looking around the fair.

When you reach your destination in a car, what follows is relatively straightforward: park, turn off ignition, remove key etc. Not so with a horse and wagon. Given the weight of the latter, it is imperative to place it where you intend it to be before taking the horse out of the shafts. Everything involved is so terribly physical: unharnessing, lifting the huge collar over the horse's head, banging in tethering posts and lugging chains.

I cherish the simple belief that getting back to basics is character-forming, especially for the children. As yet they remain unconvinced. Having settled the horse, a degree of order is now desired, something that continues to elude me. It is vital that I am organised in order to sort out the workload before dark.

Collecting water is without doubt the most important task. While it is prudent to carry a small amount on the journey, every drop we need has to be carried by hand. I send the two older children off with buckets to fetch water not only for us to drink, cook and wash in, but ten times that amount for a singularly thirsty horse. Bearing in mind that on a tether she may knock her bucket over and need it replacing, they have to make several journeys. I remind them that in order to save their energy they had better stop bellyaching. Then there is wood to gather; as it will be our only means of heating, we must have plenty.

Enough water and wood to start the day will facilitate much.

With the children gainfully employed, I set about lighting the fire. For this I snap dead twigs from branches. These are drier than any I will find lying on the ground, and within a few minutes the fire is blazing away. Traditionally the wagon would be lit with oil lamps and candles, but this is too risky with youngsters, so a good torch is our only concession to the twentieth century. With the light rapidly waning, the sooner I can get my offspring fed and into bed, the better.

At eight, six and nearly three I think my lot are a bit too young to send off into the woods with a spade or indeed use public loos unaccompanied. Instead I carefully position a gaily striped windbreak amongst the trees behind the wagon and stick a port-a-potty in the middle. The children flatly refuse to use this on account of their heads appearing above the parapet and the fear of being spotted by some passer-by. I tell them not to be so coy, while wondering how they have become so dreadfully bourgeois . . . or perhaps if I am scarring them for life.

Wagons are deceptively commodious. I sleep on the full-sized bed at the back, while my two older children occupy the cupboard beneath. The April baby is precariously balanced on a narrow bench beside the (unlit) Queenie stove. It would normally be the old and the young who slept inside, while the rest of the family would lie in the great outdoors.

There is something magical about lying in a wagon looking up at the night sky through a tiny open window. Outside I can just hear the steady grazing of my old mare and the odd rattle of her chain. The chilly air on my face is filled with the comforting smell of wood smoke and despite their earlier protestations, the children sleep soundly.

I awake at dawn and creep down the steps to greet the rising sun. Doris leaves off from her grazing to offer me the gentlest of whinnies. Last night's fire, while giving the appearance of being dead, is only teasing; the white ash may look lifeless, but how willingly a fire will spark back to life with a handful of twigs and a gentle poke, even after rain. I fill the kettle and hang it on a hook that I swing over the now dancing flames and gather up mugs as I listen for the water to boil.

Gradually, bleary-eyed children emerge from the wagon like little pupae from their cocoons. Firstly Elfina, my daughter, appears, all bare legs and wayward hair, followed by her youngest brother, Joe, who turns around gingerly to take the steep steps backwards. Then Dan, intent as always on fiddling with some vehicle he is making, absent-mindedly almost trips into the flames. They huddle round the fire for warmth, cradling mugs of steaming tea while I begin to cook a massive fry-up in the cast-iron pan. Even they enjoy this part of the day. There is no doubt that living outside gives us huge appetites and we're all as hungry as hunters.

I toast my toes by the fire. My cheeks burn while a cool breeze chills my back; the contrast exhilarates me. Going 'horse drawn' is like stepping back in time. Life slows down almost to a standstill and makes me think how much I take for granted. We quickly start to conserve water now it is no longer on tap. I smell like a kipper as I keep the fire going to boil kettles to make endless cups of tea. All the while I rabbit away to anyone who cares to listen about the joys of 'living vans'.

7

'The pan box at the back is used as a larder . . . above it is the cratch over which hangs a tilt . . . this is for storing the harness when not in use. There is room here too for a bale of hay . . . all in all they're so well thought out . . . with such a tiny amount of space things get lost quickly . . .

While I love every minute of this, I forget it is my dream exclusively. First big mistake: children do not enjoy being exhibits. Why should they? They are tired of being asked by passers-by for the umpteenth time if we are having hedgehog for supper. Instead they have rapidly become feral; they have taken to scavenging anything they can find discarded about the fairground.

I remember a woman I would not normally have credited with having anything worthwhile to impart saying the sagest thing: 'If you are lucky you will get everything you want in life. But, it won't necessarily be in the order that you would have wished for, and it certainly won't be all at the same time.'

At this juncture my marriage is in its death throes; my almost-to-be-ex-husband deigns to join us around the fire for tea. He is spotted by a friend of his, who subsequently asks:

'Who was that gypsy I saw you with at the weekend?'

'That was no gypsy, that was my *wife*!' he replies.

Chapter 2

Scene Setting

I shall endeavour to be positive. Despite the heartache of the impending divorce, I am determined to adopt a more casual approach to parenting. As I no longer have a husband to pander to, I am at last free to explore new avenues. Or so I hope.

Lest I forget, when I decided to move here, to this little cottage, I was in a complete state. It was a running away of sorts; perhaps selling up the family home was a mistake, but it's too late to dwell on that now.

I believe our neighbours have retired to this sleepy seaside village for a bit of peace and quiet. Little do they know all this is about to be shattered. They peer over the adjoining fence as I drive Doris and the wagon through the gate to our new home. With a look of horror, they watch as three filthy children spill out onto the grass.

Our little entourage has arrived!

*

I never, ever, thought my marriage would end, not in a million years. It came as a complete shock.

I was pregnant with our third child when my husband fell madly in love with someone else. I have no desire to dwell on the pain this caused, but suffice to say, we all suffered. We loved him and he loved someone else. And while I know he will always remain the children's father and hopefully see lots of them, I have to accept that the family life I had envisaged was now changed forever.

Some years earlier, my husband and I had left London for a rambling old farmhouse in Suffolk. We arrived with a copy of John Seymour's seminal book, *Self-Sufficiency*, tucked firmly under our arm. With room to indulge our love of animals and gardening, we immediately embraced a simple, country lifestyle.

This idyll was completed with the arrival of first, Elfina, and then some two and a half years later, Dan. It was about three years after that that I became pregnant with our third child, Joe.

I thought we were so happy; I certainly was.

Single parenting would never have been my first choice. I had two very close childhood friends with divorced parents, so I had first-hand knowledge of how bitterly divorce can affect young lives.

I think back to my own formative years. I believe my own parents' marriage was a happy one. My only sibling, a sister, Terry, two years my senior, was the dream child. Not only did she inherit my mother's exceptional good looks, but she was equally blessed with a kind and gentle nature. Unlike me, she was seldom at variance with our dear parents' wishes.

For my part, my happiest memories involved ponies, rivers, sea and books. I suppose therefore, with the breakdown of my marriage, it was inevitable that I should choose to move my little family back to familiar territory.

And it will be these constants, and my perennial love of books and the natural world, which will sustain me through the next phase of my life. Walks in the forests, bike rides and picnics will all play a vital role in restoring my courage. Mum is right, each day the children become a little easier.

When I was young, I would stand on the beach and gaze out to sea. I imagined I was on the brink of life, which I suppose to an extent I was. I would wonder what life held in store, what lay ahead. I no longer have time for such nonsense, I know. I know now what it's like to be out of my depth, with the shore a long way off. How I long for the safety of the coast, but that continues to elude me . . . for the moment.

I have an industrial vacuum cleaner. It's so powerful that it sucks up everything within a ten-yard radius: tiny lights off Lego cars, toy soldiers, marbles, even knickers sometimes. When the bag is full, I can't just throw it into the dustbin like any normal person. Instead I spend a very unpleasant half-hour groping meticulously through the most horrible mess in the hope of retrieving some of the lost objects. It has just occurred to me: could this be the thrust of my whole problem – a microcosm of my life, as it were? Always groping through mess, be it physical or mental, in search of lost treasures, instead of accepting they are gone and applying myself to the next thing.

Chapter 3

What Doesn't Kill Me

What an extraordinary year it has been. There have been so many emotions, and so very much pain. I console myself that things may never be quite as bad again. What does not kill me makes me stronger.

I feel in my pocket for an old luggage label. It is the only tangible thing that remains of my father. We knew he was dying; he was diagnosed with cancer some two years ago. And although we thought we were prepared, it still came as a shock. With hindsight I now think it a privilege to be forewarned. Although I was devastated when I first learnt of his illness, it did prepare me; it allowed me to deal with the mourning process while he lived. When I had overcome the sadness, it left me free to enjoy every precious minute I could with him.

I look at the writing on the label and smile.

And now he is dead, but I don't always remember. I hear a joke or a little story I know he will love and just as I am about to phone him it all comes flooding back. So instead, I will my thoughts up into the ether and blow him a kiss. I still feel him about me, I can still hear his laugh.

He would have loved this little cottage with its proximity to the sea and now he will never see it.

He was a gentle man, a kind and a caring father. It would have broken his heart to know that Ben had left not only me but his own children. It would be beyond his comprehension that any father could behave so. Knowing how very unwell he was and not wishing to distress him further, my mother and I made a joint decision that he should never know. And he never did.

So within the space of a mere few months, life as I knew it has been completely upended. And while I might wish to grieve for a lost father and a wrecked marriage, it is evident there will be little time to indulge such emotion.

I knew the moment I walked into this little cottage that it was for us. I made an offer and it was accepted within twenty-four hours. Perhaps on reflection I was a tad too hasty in my decision. There was no survey done and no thinking; it was simply a visceral, knee-jerk reaction based on first impressions.

The door key is substantial and makes a satisfying clunk as I unlock the kitchen door onto the heap of boxes left by the removal men. The children push past me and rush off down the corridor. In the sitting room there are more packing cases and our old grey Chesterfield is the only place, apart from the floor, I can see to sit down. Not that there will be much time for that, given the piles of cases to be unpacked.

But I'm tired and hungry, as are the children, and the horse needs my attention. In my eagerness to buy this seaside idyll, I omitted to notice there wasn't actually room for a horse. But I'll think about that one tomorrow. For now I tether her in the back garden and set about finding something to feed the children.

The previous owners appear to have taken the cooker; it didn't occur to me to discuss such things at the time. I gaze at the place where it should be and instead notice peeling paint and layers of grease. The reality of my new situation is gradually dawning on me.

Upstairs the beds have been put up but are unmade. Typically, I have forgotten to label the boxes so it is a complete mystery to me as to which ones may or may not contain the bedding. And while the children suggest we play *Eeni, Meeni, Mini Mo,* I am in no mood for guessing games. The light is waning and my heart is dull. How much easier and reassuring it would be if we all slept in the wagon tonight instead; after all, I know where everything is in there, especially some biscuits.

We are huddled together in the wagon eating cold baked beans and chocolate digestives when we hear voices. There is a knock, then a quizzical face appears over the half door.

'Hallo,' it says, 'I'm Dick, and this is Audrey. We're your new neighbours.'

I smile, while trying to push the April baby under the bunk bed as I haven't had time to change him and his nappy hangs off.

'We were wondering if there is anything we can do to help?' he continues.

'Gosh, that's so kind, but we're fine thanks, honest. I'm Nicky, by the way and these are my three children . . .'

'Do you have a television?' asks Dan.

'Shh!' I whisper, trying to gag him.

'We're not allowed it,' he continues, 'and I want to watch *Doctor Who.*'

'Oh shut up, Dan, this is far more fun. We like to make our own amusement,' I say, in a rather superior way. 'Please don't listen to him.'

'Well, if there's anything you need, we're only over the fence.'

'Thanks, but we're just fine,' I say.

'Oh, and by the way . . . how long do you intend to keep the horse in the garden for?' asks Dick, as he turns to leave.

'Till she's eaten all the grass or I can find some grazing close by,' I say. 'Why do you ask?'

'Just wondered. Goodnight,' he says. 'Come on, Audrey.'

'What nice neighbours,' I think to myself as I tuck the children up.

Chapter 4

An Englishman's Home

For someone who hates house-hunting, I have done my fair share.

My initial ticklist for our new home included a field for Doris, space for a vegetable garden and being miles from everyone and anyone. I was determined to distance myself from life. The house itself was secondary, but if there was a choice I would prefer something old.

Apart from the latter, Bramley Cottage ticks none of these boxes. But I knew from the moment I drove down the hill and smelt the sea air, knew when I turned the corner and actually caught a glimpse of the sea, knew even before I picked my way through its overly planted cottage garden, complete with a wishing well, that I could live here. And more importantly, could live here with my children and our assortment of pets.

I had seen an advertisement for it in the Sunday papers. I immediately phoned and viewed it on the Monday. The owners, an elderly couple, were marketing it themselves and so, in the absence of an estate agent, I made them an offer and was accepted there and then.

Far from being remote, the cottage is a Victorian semi-detached and stands in the main street of a tiny hamlet on the Suffolk coast. The little village is made up of less than seventy houses, mainly huddled together in two lots. It is to prove strangely reassuring, this proximity of others. On long winter nights, when the light goes so early, I wonder how I could possibly have coped with young children miles from any other beings.

The cottage itself is ideal. My priority is to create a home for the children that I can run singlehandedly.

The front door leads into a small hallway with a room on either side. Along a very dark corridor is the bathroom and next to that the kitchen. The elderly owners had used one of the downstairs rooms as a bedroom, hence the bathroom. At first I found it quite disconcerting, given there were three further bedrooms upstairs. But in time it has grown to be one of the features I love best. Bathtime with youngsters can be a lengthy affair and it can also conflict with homework, teatime and all the other activities – a bathroom next to the kitchen means I can stick the children in the bath and simply walk next door to the kitchen and cook their tea. They are close enough to keep an eye on and an ear out for while I get on with other things.

Beyond the kitchen there was originally a small room, quite obviously converted from one of the adjoining out-buildings, which was used as a dining room. From the moment I saw it I had plans to knock down the wall and make one huge kitchen.

The garden to the front of the house is mainly flowerbeds. There is an unmade drive, enough for two or three cars, and a garage that is too small for anything except our motley assortment of bikes.

The garden is so overplanted that the spectacular views from the bottom are completely obscured. The previous owners were quite obviously keen gardeners: I know that she was also a flower arranger. To this end the back garden came stuffed with every conceivable shrub, the majority of which had been chosen for their form, or colour, in a vase. There were several varieties of berberis and while I love their autumn colour, their thorns are vicious in the extreme. This we learn the hard way while playing hide and seek, so I decide they will be the first to come out. A field for Doris was high on my list, but tethered between these shrubs is to be her lot until I can find some proper grazing to rent.

I can remember the first bedroom I had all to myself; until then I had always shared with my older sister, Terry. I presume she had had a say in the decorations because they certainly weren't to my taste. There were a deal of frills and flowers, if I recall correctly, and it had a decidedly girly feel to it.

If an Englishman's home is his castle, my first bedroom was my fortress. While the walls were painted a pale mushroomy colour, not my choice, the shelves and furniture were a bright sunny yellow; my favourite. The Thelwell pony theme I so longed for on my new curtains would have to wait; there was still a deal of wear to be had from the old ones. But I didn't really mind. I could shut the door on the world and lose myself in a book. I began my first library and numbered the books accordingly. *Black Beauty*, my all-time favourite, was number one; then there was *Wind in the Willows, Heidi, Little Women* . . . For reasons I have never understood I was not allowed to read Enid Blyton. I thought it an odd decision even then. Not only are they rollicking good stories but they are the logical progression from strip comics where the narrative is supported by pictures. For me, however, not being allowed really meant not being caught.

I had a friend at school whose mother was quite obviously more broad-minded than the persistently domineering variety that had fallen to me. As I walked past her house on the way home from school, I would borrow another volume of the *Famous Five* or *Secret Seven* with a promise to return it on my way to school in the morning. Now that I had no sibling to consider I could read late into the night, and I always did. So began my lifelong passion for books. My other constant in those far off days was anything equine. On the gaily painted shelves not given over to my books was a burgeoning collection of china horses.

The room was most definitely mine and I loved it.

In this knowledge that a bedroom should be sacrosanct, I am determined that my children will feel an equal sense of control in their own chosen space.

Upstairs in the cottage are three bedrooms and a little washroom. The end room, which is Elfie's, while smaller than the others, has by far the best view. Out across the grazing marshes you can see towards Sole Bay and beyond. And there is the comforting beam of the Southwold lighthouse as it flashes reassuringly through the night.

I have an abiding dislike of choice. It confuses me. I would rather have little or none. With no choice, I simply roll up my sleeves and get on with it, or take what's in front of me and make the best of it. Conversely, while I struggle to choose what I do like, I always know precisely what I don't. According to my mother, this is already halfway there. I'm not so sure. I am fascinated, therefore, when my daughter displays a decisiveness that has always eluded me. She knows in an instant which colour and curtains she wants for her new bedroom. It's just as well this is to be exclusively hers; Dan's reaction on seeing pink walls and flower fairy curtains provokes a fight. They roll about on the floor like puppies.

'Yuk, pink. It's gross,' he says, between pulling hair and appropriate faces.

Within a matter of days Elfie has transformed her little domain into a fairy grotto.

Her collection of My Little Ponies is almost obscene: Dream Palace with its turrets and swimming pool, My Little Grooming parlour and so on . . . But she is in her element and I have to remind myself that it is her space. However, I must inquire at the toy shop if they make a My Little Knackers Yard.

The boys are to share a room initially. They are still of an age when they don't mind what colours the walls are. This makes life much simpler for me as I paint it magnolia along with every other room in the house. What floor space remains between the two little beds is quickly eclipsed by Lego and Star Wars vehicles. That this will obviate any future hope of vacuuming crosses my mind, but again I am resolute: this is their very own little sanctuary.

My room is almost Spartan by comparison. I look at the cast-iron double bed that takes up the major part of it and wonder whether it was sentiment or optimism that made me hang onto it. I have two windows, both with rather indifferent views. I'm uncertain as to whether I can be overlooked by our immediate neighbours, but after some thought I decide I don't give a damn. I know this cottage is right for us.

The corridor linking the front hall to the kitchen at the back is long enough to be almost pitch-black. I have an old cast-iron cathedral heater in which I put a red light bulb and leave it on permanently. Not only does this radiate a gentle warmth down the almost dark passage but, as a friend comments, it symbolises the heart of our new home.

Chapter 5

Mother

Before I have a chance to unpack and knock our new home into some semblance of order, my recently widowed mother phones to announce that she plans a visit.

I know I should be pleased, grateful even, that she is taking an interest in our new life so soon. But there is a nagging undertone.

Struggle as I may, I never quite manage to get it right with Mum; but this will not hinder me from trying to make this visit a new beginning for us all.

To this end, I make redecorating the guest room a priority. It is not in my nature to look for trouble – I would sooner open a book. However, this is the first property I have bought completely on my own. Only now, with the previous occupants' furniture gone, the rooms take on an altogether different appearance. I begin to see the cracks; well, not so much the cracks as damp. The outside walls in this little bedroom are full of it, and with my mum's impending visit, there is no time to deal with it now. So I paper over the worst bits and push a chest of drawers in front to hide it.

The children are excited about our first visitor and do as much to help as they can. Elfie has the sweetest nature and already her artistic side is beginning to show. I give her the task of picking flowers for Ganti's room. I remember reading an old-fashioned book that said to always remember the three Bs when you have visitors: Books in case they are bored, Blankets in case they are cold and Biscuits in case they are hungry.

Dan's contribution is to keep Joe amused while Elfie and I see to the finishing touches. Finally, I stand back and admire our new guest room. The wallpaper looks suitably old-fashioned with its little pink rose buds. Not that anything so twee would necessarily have been my first choice, but knowing how essential appearances are to my mother, I am actually thrilled with the results. I've made some patchwork curtains and even managed to work in some of the pale pinks and greens of the walls. The leaded windows and the stone floors, particular to this period of cottage, complete the almost saccharin décor. But I console myself that Mum will love it; it's important to me that she does.

The Elf is becoming such a help. I am mindful that it will be all too easy to put on her given her good nature; she positively delights in all things domestic. We make a tin of fork biscuits for Mum's room, while the boys are in the next room painting cards to welcome her.

The room beside the kitchen has lost its status of dining room and is gradually metamorphosing into a one-size-fits-all sort of room. There is an open fire and a table big and old enough for the children to make as much mess as they like. Despite the walls being even damper than the spare bedroom

– the paper is actually hanging off in places – I have no more time to camouflage it before Mum's imminent arrival.

Her train gets in at six. The children are not really old enough to leave on their own. I'm uncertain as to the age when it is actually legal. Or indeed, what age my daughter must be before I can pay her to keep the boys in order. Another fallout from the divorce: I can no longer dash off and do what I want in the knowledge the children are safe with the other parent. I find I have to now plan things in advance. Not something that comes naturally to someone of my impetuous nature.

I cannot miss my mother at the station.

I suppose I have always known I was not the child my mother wanted. I forgave her; there was nothing else I could do. Some say we choose the family we are born into. If that is so, it was my first big mistake.

How do you cope with a mother christened Mona Lisa? A woman to whom beauty was, is and ever shall be, her driving force? She was the youngest daughter of eccentric artists, too impoverished (or careless) to bathe her in the milk of human kindness. Not that such a dunking would have necessarily predisposed her to loving something less than perfect, but it may have been worth a try. As I said, I understood this – it was her default setting.

So it is with mixed emotions that I stand on the station platform awaiting her arrival. Of course I am excited about seeing her; I am longing to show her our new home, explore the surrounding countryside. Perhaps she might even have brought her paints. I so want her to love it as much as I already do. But as always there is the nagging certainty that, however hard I might try to please, something beyond my control will spoil it. I beam, *Please may we not be at variance, just this once, please,* up into the evening sky and watch as the train comes to a halt.

I have an abiding image of my mother in a hat, and true to form she does not disappoint. As a child I always found it a bit embarrassing, but now I see it does have its advantages. As the train comes to a standstill and the doors are flung open, I see a tall, elegant woman with a big floppy felt hat step out onto the platform.

I run towards her, 'Here, give me your bags,' I say, leaning forward and giving her a kiss. 'How wonderful to see you.' I'm delighted to see she has brought paints and an easel.

'Where are the children?' she asks immediately.

'I've left them at home. Why?'

'You've done what? Do you have a baby-sitter already?'

'No,' I say. 'Elfie is keeping an eye on the boys. They were all playing so happily I didn't want to mess up their game.'

'Well, I think that's thoroughly irresponsible. I thought you'd have known better than to leave children of that age alone.'

'Oh Mum, please don't start. The cottage is only four miles away; we'll be home in a tick.'

'I don't care how many miles away it might be, you simply can't leave young children alone.'

'And it's not irresponsible of Ben to leave all of us?' I shout. 'I was only doing what I thought would be best for the children.'

'The sooner you get one thing straight, young lady, the better. Whatever Ben has done is his business and must no longer concern you. Two wrongs don't make a right. From now on you put the children first.'

'But can't you see that's precisely why I left them playing,' I say as I start up the car.

I drive on in silence, determined not to row.

'Nearly here, Mum. Look you can just glimpse the sea . . . look . . . just over there.'

As I pull into the drive, the Elf rushes to the door to meet us.

'Ganti! Come and see your new room,' she says excitedly, taking my mother's hand.

'Where are the boys?' I ask, as I follow them along the corridor.

'They're here, in here,' says Elfie, pushing open the door. 'They're playing a game.'

On the floor in front of me is Dan with a collar around his neck, while Joe holds a lead and drags him about. Dan stops beside the tin of fork biscuits I had placed on my mother's bedside table, then sits up on his haunches in a begging sort of a way.

'I'm your dog,' he says to Joe, 'and now you must feed me.'

Joe proceeds to open the tin and pop a biscuit, the last one I notice, into his big brother's mouth. 'Good boy,' he says. 'Good boy,' and pats him on the head.

'Darlings, come on, get up off the floor, come and give Ganti a big hug,' I say.

'I thought you didn't let the children have sweet things. If you remember I never allowed you or Terry to have them when you were young. Empty calories, rot your teeth,' says my mother in a rather imperious manner.

I remember only too well how we were denied sweets.

Chapter 6

Thou Shalt Not Steal

🖋 Nellie's shop was an Aladdin's cave. And while I hadn't a clue what an Aladdin's cave was or should be, I was mindful that it was very special. A little bell hung on the back of the door and tinkled every time it opened. As if by magic Nellie appeared from nowhere, shuffled past bags of flour and kindling, and stuck her head through an arch of wares. With her halo of fishing hooks, drawing pins, chalk and fuses she would peer down at me. What was really magic though was sometimes she had no teeth and then sometimes she did . . . she moved them about. I couldn't do that with mine.

The shop was tiny, four paces at most between door and counter, but what a counter! I was just tall enough to see over the top and gaze at the chaos behind. There was chaos before as well, albeit organised. Narrow shelves lined the walls, stacked high with tins and dried things; I had no idea what the names meant, but they were just the ticket to practise my reading skills on if I had to wait.

There was a ledge on the front of the counter especially for sweets, square wooden boxes with glass lids, full of everything I wasn't allowed: sherbet dabs, flying saucers, gobstoppers, sugar mice, jelly babies, and best of all, liquorice. Every time I ran an errand, there *they* would be winking at me.

My mother wouldn't let us have sweets. Fruit or nuts were deemed quite adequate as treats. 'You don't want to end up with teeth like Nellie's now do you?' This is the same woman who would end up sending her loving daughters hundreds of miles away to school, reasoning that all girls educated in Scotland ended up with huge bottoms from playing too much hockey.

She kept a pot of money on her desk, a small pot, but money all the same. With hindsight, I think it thoroughly irresponsible of her to leave such temptation in my path.

And I was tempted. Half a crown is a fine-looking coin and also very pocketable; as such I nicked one.

I waited until the coast was clear: Mother invariably retired after lunch, Mrs Wilson, Mum's help, had gone home and the afternoon stretched out before me.

I pushed my hand into my shorts pocket and pulled out the huge stolen coin. As I ran my finger around its edge, I imagined all I could buy with it. Anything in the world, I thought.

My world had yet to extend beyond Nellie's, certainly on my own. It was only a short walk, involving no crossings of roads but over an old granite bridge, and as such deemed safe.

So, as my mother rested and the bees hummed, I crept out of the gate and headed off towards the shop.

It always took both of my hands to turn the shiny brass handle and push the door open. The bell jingled to alert Nellie, who duly shuffled out and stuck her head through the frame of life's necessities.

I stood on tiptoes and placed my money on the wooden counter.

'Was it something for your mother youse wanted?' she asked in her broad Scottish accent.

I shook my head as I pushed the coin further across towards her.

'Liquorice,' I just managed to whisper, glancing furtively around the empty shop.

'Aye, it's there in front of you, just help yersel.'

'But please,' I stuttered, 'can I have that much?'

'What d'ya mean, *that* much?'

'As much as that,' I said, touching the coin. 'As much as that will get me.'

'Are you sure? Half a crown'll buy you an awful lot. Do you ken how many pennies are in that?' she said.

Again I shook my head. I stared down at the box of shiny lengths of liquorice once more.

Then to my horror she continued, 'And where did a wee one like you get such a big piece of money? Yer Mother usually puts things down in the book.'

Now, given this was my first venture into a life of crime, I hadn't anticipated lying as well as thieving. I felt the colour rise in my cheeks.

'I'm having a party, it's for my friends,' I said, surprised at my own invention. 'I want that much,' I repeated again, having already decided if this didn't work I would do a runner.

'Very well then, but I'll have to wrap it up. There'll be too much to go in a bag.'

I watched her smooth out a huge piece of brown paper on the counter. Then she waddled round to the front and lifted up the entire wooden box of liquorice. I had never seen her lower half before and was captivated by the size of her backside.

'Are you good at your sums?' she asked, breaking into my reverie.

'No, not really.' I glanced towards the door.

'You can help me count. There are twelve pennies in a shilling and you get four sticks for one penny. How many do you think that will make?'

I smiled inanely, willing her to just get on and count them herself, and quickly.

'There, there's forty-eight. Now . . . another forty-eight.' She began counting once more. 'This is a great deal of liquorice; you must have a lot of friends. Only another twenty-four to go . . . are you sure you wanted this much?'

Strangely my initial excitement at being the mistress of such wealth was rapidly waning, to be replaced with what I can only describe as mild panic. I was transfixed by the quantity of liquorice piling up, quite literally, before my eyes. I willed her to stop but it was no good.

'One hundred and six, one hundred and seven, one hundred . . .' The drone of her voice, mingled with the buzzing of a big meat fly, had a hypnotic effect.

'There we are, one hundred and twenty sticks of liquorice,' she said. 'I'll have to order some more.' She began to wrap the stiff paper into an oblong parcel and tied it up neatly with a length of string.

'Now will you be able to carry it? It's quite heavy, mind,' she said, bringing it around to where I was standing. She placed it in my outstretched arms. 'Are you going to manage?' she asked, holding the door open as I struggled out with my illicit goods.

I heard the faint jingle of the bell as the door closed behind me and suddenly I felt very alone.

On the other side of the bridge from the shop was a steep path down to the river. I kicked off my sandals and skidded down. Under the bridge was a stone ledge. It was just the place for dangling feet in the water and watching minnows dart about. Here it was cool, away from the searing heat of the afternoon, a place to think. I sat down and placed the parcel beside me. I stared at it and it stared back at me.

I thought of my mother. She would probably be up by now and I wondered how I could possibly explain all this away. Where could I put it? *Under my bed*? But Mrs Wilson was always cleaning, she'd be sure to discover it. *Could I confide in her, I wondered?* No, she would go straight to my mother. Cupboards were equally vulnerable, some nosey parker would find it and questions would be asked.

I unwrapped my precious bundle and gazed at the contents. I picked up a stick of my favourite sweet and took a bite. It tasted sour, I spat it out, unable to swallow even one mouthful. Then, one by one, I started to throw my treasured booty into the still, running water. I watched as some floated down in the current while others sank slowly to the riverbed. Shoals of minnows darted towards them and I truly willed them to enjoy the feast that I had missed out on.

I couldn't resist taking another mouthful from the last solitary piece. It also tasted bitter so I hurled what remained far out across the water. I folded the paper and shoved the string deep into my pocket.

Once home I crept to my mother's desk and placed the paper in one of the drawers, the string in the string box and lastly I pushed the pot of loose change to the very back – out of sight.

'Oh, there you are, darling. I've been looking for you everywhere.' My mother's voice behind me made me jump. 'I

Chapter 7

Never Explain

Breakfast. We are all seated around the kitchen table tucking into freshly laid eggs.

'Whatever is that outside the window?' Mum asks.

'Front or back?' I say in an overly jocular manner. I'd been wondering how long it would take her to notice our brightly painted wagon parked in the middle of the front lawn. It has crossed my mind to lie, to pretend it was someone else's. But in truth I have always found fibbing required a degree of mental alacrity that somehow eluded me; I find it simpler to be honest. Under the circumstances it is just as well. Before I have a chance to explain, Dan pipes up, 'It's our new wagon and we can all fit in, we've just come back from a steam fair with it.'

'And we've got the horse to pull it,' chipped in the Elf, pulling my mother by the hand. 'She's called Doris and she's tied up in the back garden. Come and look, come on, Ganti.'

While I knew she would notice the bow top as soon as she opened her bedroom curtains, I had hoped I would have time to discuss the small matter of the horse with Mum leisurely, as it were. But the children in their eagerness to share this new addition to our family have completely blown any chance I might have had of softening the news.

The boys and I follow Elfie and Mum out of the back door and down the garden. Doris leaves off from her grazing and gives a gentle whinny.

'Isn't she lovely, Mum,' I say, giving Doris an apple. 'She's a real wagon horse. Look at her mane. Isn't she a dream? She's even coloured . . .'

'What do you mean by coloured, darling?'

'It's an expression; a term for a black and white, or brown and white horse, and she's got the most wonderful temperament.'

'I can see that,' says my mother, as the boys start a sword fight with some old branches and whack Doris on her flank by mistake. She doesn't even flinch.

'No, she is lovely,' says Mum, giving her a pat. 'But surely you're not planning to keep her here. Look, she's already eaten that shrub . . . and barked that tree; the garden will be ruined in no time. I would have thought the neighbours will complain too. Have you asked them if they mind?

'Well, not exactly,' I say, recalling the look of horror on Dick's face when he first saw her. 'It's just I haven't really had a chance to find any proper grazing yet.' While thinking, *Good old Mum. Trust you to hit the nail on the head.*

We return to the kitchen enveloped in a silence that speaks volumes. Fortunately the children are clamouring for attention and I have already mooted a good blustery walk along the cliffs. By the time we have donned the layers of woollies and boots so vital for the biting winds we are about to encounter, the conversation has resumed at a less flammable level. But the day is still young.

34

Later, I light a big cosy fire in the room that adjoins the kitchen. As I cook supper I take pleasure in listening to my mother as she reads to my newly scrubbed brood. They have had a fine day of it; they are tired with all the fresh air and it won't be long before they are tucked up in bed. But my heart is already sinking at the turn the conversation will inevitably take once my mother and I are on our own.

'Oh it's so lovely to have you here, Mum,' I say wrapping my arms around her and giving her a hug. 'How are you managing without Bumpa?'

'I'm fine, thank you, but it does get a bit lonely at times. To be honest though, after such a long illness it's almost a relief that he's dead. I was worn out,' she says with an admirable candour. 'But darling, don't worry about me, it's you I want to talk about.'

Here goes, I think, getting up from the table to fetch my tobacco. 'Let's have a glass of wine,' I suggest. 'I could kill for one.'

I can feel my mother's eyes on me as I roll a cigarette.

'I thought you'd given that dreadful habit up,' she says. 'You've no idea how unattractive you look when you inhale . . . and the smell!'

'Mum please, at least I try not to smoke in front of the children. I'd love to give it up but things are a bit stressful at the mo. I'll do it one day, honest.' I push a glass of wine across the table towards her.

'Thank you,' she says, taking a sip. 'Now tell me, what's all this nonsense with the wagon. It must have cost a fortune. You led me to believe you had no money. I've been wracking my brains wondering what I can do to help and I come here . . . and find this!'

I drag deeply on my fag. I'm half prepared for this so I've

already thought of quite a plausible answer; to try and turn the tables as it were.

'Mum,' I begin. 'Do you remember when I was small you embroidered me a little picture? I loved it, I still do. Can you remember what it said?'

'Of course I can, it said *Follow your Dreams*. But I don't see what on earth this has got to do with the wagon, or the horse for that matter.'

'You honestly can't see? My whole life has just fallen apart. My husband's buggered off and my father has just died. Can't you see I have to have a dream? I have to have something for me, otherwise I'll go nuts. It may only be a wagon to you but I can't explain how my heart soars when I simply look at it . . .'

Before I can say any more, Mum raises her hand, 'Calm down, please Nicky. Don't be so dramatic. You know I can't stand all this emotion. Anyone would think you were the only wronged woman in the world.'

'Pull yourself together,' she continues. 'All I'm asking is how you can possibly afford a horse and wagon in your present circumstances. I would have thought, judging by the state of this place, you had more important things to spend your money on.'

'What do you mean, don't you like the cottage?' I say defensively. 'Mum, I'm in my thirties; surely it's up to me what I do with my life. I didn't choose to be a single mother but, now that I am, I'm going to make the best of it, and if that involves taking a more relaxed attitude to parenting so be it. You know Bumpa left Terry and me a little money. Well, I've spent mine on the one thing I've always dreamed of. Please try to understand.'

I get up to refill her glass. 'Let's change the subject, shall we? I want you to help me sort out the children's bedrooms in the morning. I see you've brought your paints.'

As I lie in bed later that night, I think over our conversations. I genuinely don't think I consciously try to upset my mother, yet quite obviously I do. Try as I may, I continue to get it wrong.

I have an abiding memory of buying her a pair of slippers for Christmas. Where I got the money from heaven alone knows; most probably I nicked it. However, her reaction verged on the manic. She flew into a violent rage and screamed at me; did I not know how she abhorred slippers, had never worn them nor had her mother even allowed them in the house. People who wore slippers were sloppy, undisciplined; slippers induced a feeling of inertia and made one lazy . . .

Even as a child I found this thinking bizarre. But I still don't own a pair.

Against the odds, I awake the next morning enveloped in a kind of warmth. As I dress, I remember Mum is staying. Despite our little variances the night before, it is wonderful to have her with us even for such a fleeting visit.

Over breakfast we discuss the day. Doris is in need of some exercise and I feel it would be good for everyone if I take myself off for a bracing ride while leaving Mum a free rein with her grandchildren.

My strategy works a treat. Not only do I return invigorated, but as I climb the stairs and peer into the boys' room, there is my mother painting beetles and insects all around their window sill.

'Please, Ganti. Can I have worms there?' asks my embryonic naturalist.

'Of course, Joe,' says my mother, 'just let me finish this

branch. And then you must tell me what birds you would like on it.'

Dan, I notice, has his own little palette of paint and is completely engrossed in decorating the wall beside his bed with aliens and spaceships.

I tiptoe along the corridor and look into the Elf's room. She is balanced precariously on top of her wardrobe painting fairies on the ceiling.

'Darling, those are magical, did you do them yourself?'

'Some of them,' she says. 'But Ganti showed me how. She's going to help me muriel the whole room when she's finished Joe's window.'

This is the mother I wanted; this is the one I love.

Chapter 8

Pets and Neighbours

In addition to Doris the horse, we arrived at our new home with Sidney and Toots, two bantams belonging to the children. They are the most comical-looking pair I have ever set eyes on.

However, despite being tame, they are flatly refusing to return to the little shed I have allocated them as their very own *des res*. Instead they would rather roost on the uppermost branches of an overgrown Pyracantha. I only mention the name of their chosen perch to demonstrate to those who know about such things why I fail to extricate them. The density of the branches and the ferocity of the thorns negates any hope in hell of me climbing up (after dusk I might add) to catch the little buggers. I've tried, I really have. Once I actually managed to catch Sidney's leg and gave it a tug but he let out such an alarming squawk that I let go immediately and fell out of the tree.

I don't really have a problem with Sidney and Toots preferring to live al fresco. It's my neighbours, Dick and Audrey, the ones who I stupidly refer to as the nosey neighbours. The alliteration appeals to the boys and I am mortified to hear them running around the garden chanting, 'Nosey neighbours, nosey neighbours.'

I genuinely confused their initial interest in our less than conventional arrival as kindly concern. Now, I'm not so sure. They have a tendency to turn up on the doorstep a little too frequently; often with gifts of sweets for the children or vegetables for me. When I open the door and don't ask them in, they sort of lurk. 'Where do your chickens sleep?' Dick enquires one morning.

'Oh, they're not chickens, they're bantams, Barbu D'Uccles actually,' I say pedantically.

'Aren't they adorable,' I continue, as Sidney and Toots strut past. 'I had hoped they would like it in there,' I say, pointing to the old chicken shed. 'But they prefer roosting outside.'

'That's precisely what I'm getting at. They're a damned nuisance. That cockerel starts crowing well before daylight. It's driving Audrey mad, she can't get a wink of sleep.'

'I'm so sorry, I've tried to catch them, I really have, but they just keep going higher and higher up the tree. I've tried shutting them up for a few days but that doesn't work either,' I say, genuinely apologetically.

I am digging up another evil-thorned berberis in the back garden when Dick appears as if from nowhere.

'That's a fine shrub you're digging out. Pity really, Jean took a great pride in her planting.'

'I'm sure she did,' I say defensively. 'But it's hardly a child-friendly garden, these thorns are lethal. Dan got one stuck in his head yesterday – it was quite nasty; could have gone in his eye. I intend to clear quite a few of these shrubs to make room for the children to play.'

'Tell me,' he continues, 'how long do you intend to keep that bonfire going?'

'Don't know really. Suppose till this lot is all gone,' I say, pointing to a heap of pee-soaked old carpet I'd pulled up off the bathroom floor.

'It's just we have guests staying and the smoke is blowing right through our sitting-room window,' he says.

'Gosh, I'm so sorry. Why didn't you say so straight away?'

'Also, Audrey and I were wondering just how many more animals you intend to keep in your garden?' says Dick.

Actually, I would quite like to know myself, knowing how much the children love them. 'There's just Rose,' I say cheerfully. 'I'm rather hoping to collect her this weekend.'

'And who, or what, is Rose, if I may ask?'

'Rose,' I say, 'Rose is a very important member of the family; she's our donkey!'

And with that, I bid him good afternoon and head back into the house. I think back to the Christmas I bought Rose. It seems like another lifetime ago, before all of this.

Years ago a traveller I knew called at the farm. Although he dealt mainly in carpets, I had bought the odd thing off him in the past. I followed him out to his van to see what useless thing I could possibly live without this time. And there in the back, all eyes and ears, lay a little donkey foal.

Christmas was on the horizon and I thought she would make the most perfect present for the children. Already I could picture her lying in front of a blazing fire on Christmas morning, surrounded by tinsel and a great deal of excitement.

I chose not to remember the words of 'Uncle Jack', one of the finest horsemen in the county, that a donkey's only use was to teach children to swear.

Not until she was paid for did it occur to me it was still

November, and how was I going to keep such a secret from a seven-, a three- and one-year-old who all firmly believed in Santa. Fortunately I managed to persuade a good friend to 'hide' her for me. Then, late on Christmas Eve, I collected the little moke and popped her into a stable while the children slept, gloriously unaware of my surprise!

On Christmas morning I rose especially early, before the chaos of the day embraced us all. My plan was to put the donkey in the sitting room . . . casually among the presents.

Donkeys have a reputation for being stubborn. In their defence, I always used to argue that it was quite simply bad handling; if you got them young enough and treated them firmly they would be no problem at all. I no longer believe this. They are without doubt the most obstinate, single-minded cussed creatures on God's earth. As I tried, and failed, to coax her through the back door I remembered Uncle Jack's words. However hard I pushed, shoved or proffered food, it was all for nothing. She would not budge over the doorstep. I decided to tie her up to a rose bush outside the window.

The children tumbled down the stairs in various stages of undress still rubbing sleep from their eyes. They rushed into the sitting room and gasped with delight when they saw their stockings brimming over with goodies. I was unsure as to who was more excited and simply couldn't contain myself.

'Oh my goodness,' I feigned, pointing towards the window. 'Whatever is that out there? Look . . . tied to the rose bush . . . can you see?' I picked up the April baby and carried him in the direction of the window. 'Good heavens! What has Santa left?'

The other children rushed after me and, standing on tip-toes, peered through the frosty glass.

We christened her Christmas Rose and she is now well

and truly an established member of the family. She can be difficult, bolshie, but charming sometimes; whatever takes her fancy. I bought some harness and a little cart so that she could take us all out on adventures. The children also ride her and when she's had enough of them she quite simply pitches them off. For that I respect her! But there is no doubt; she is an enormous bonus to our family life.

One evening, sometime later, I overheard the children talking.

'Who asked Santa for a donkey in the first place?' asked the Elf.

I stood riveted on the other side of the door.

'Well it certainly wasn't me because I don't even like horses. I asked for a *Millennium Falcon*,' said Dan predictably. 'And I didn't get it.'

'I know then, it must have been my fault,' said the Elf. 'I asked for a My Little Pony. Perhaps he just got it wrong!'

Chapter 9

Newcomers

As I draw my bedroom curtains, I look out beyond our fence to the nosey neighbours' immaculate newly built home. I've had time to ruminate on the recent goings on and in truth, perhaps I have been less than thoughtful. It must be disappointing to retire to your dream home only to find us lot as your new neighbours.

In the other half of our semi-detached cottage lives a dear little bright-eyed lady with a ready smile.

It seems Emmi has lived in the village, and indeed the same cottage, all her life: from childhood, through married life, and now to widowhood.

Now, while I'm not trying to perpetrate the nosey neighbour theme, living in such close proximity I cannot fail to notice the regular pattern to her daily life. At first light I see her walking down to unlock the church with her little sausage dog trotting faithfully by her side. On Mondays, without fail, she hangs out her washing. There is little evidence of her for the rest of the morning but, if the weather is fair, her afternoons are invariably spent gardening; sometimes in her impossibly pretty front garden with its ancient apple tree and cottage-style borders, or, from an upstairs window, I can just see her working on a not insubstantial vegetable garden. Even now as the year draws to a close and the weather is sometimes fierce, I can spot her digging and mulching. There are rows of healthy-looking brassicas and leeks all bordered by some late flowering dahlias and it is such a comforting sight.

There is no evidence of Emmi owning a car, and with no village shop, I assume she must be highly organised. On a Thursday, without fail, she is picked up by an equally elderly friend and is driven to the nearest town, where I presume she does her only shopping for the week.

To say she reminds me of a favourite character from a much-loved children's book would be to belittle her perhaps, but she does. But she is the last person in the world I would ever wish to belittle. I find it deeply reassuring to have such an unobtrusive neighbour. And now, with the nights drawing in so quickly, I wonder again how I ever could have imagined living miles from anywhere.

While 'drive' is probably too grand a word for the bit of front garden on which we park the car, there is a five-bar gate at the entrance that frankly has seen better days. I rarely close it on account of its state of dilapidation. I blame the children for this; they will keep swinging on it. Actually, it's a fairly harmless pastime and I can keep a safe eye on them from the kitchen as I watch a selection of them lean over the top bar while one of the others gives it a mighty push and away they go, backwards and forwards, laughing their heads off. Given the amount of innocent pleasure they so obviously derive from something so puerile, I see little point in stopping them.

The house opposite to ours is in an elevated position and as such it and its occupants look down on us. I am doing a spot of weeding one day when the male of the household crosses the road and approaches me.

'May I have a word?' he says in an overly ostentatious manner.

I look up and give him a broad smile, 'Of course.'

'I just want to say that the view from our house and garden is without parallel.'

Pompous fart, I think, while agreeing that it must indeed be wonderful.

'I can stand in my front garden and gaze out over your little cottage to the marshes and the sea beyond,' he continues.

'I can imagine it must be a lovely view. We have one like that from a back bedroom,' I say, wondering where all this is going.

'The thing is, Nicky, as I say, that's when I gaze out. It's when I gaze down and see your garden, the gate hanging off its hinges, the mess, your children running about half naked like little street urchins. It spoils the view entirely.'

I am not going to rise to this. I made up my mind to be on good terms with all around me. I can see no mileage in ruffling feathers; who knows when we might have need of one another. But somehow my good intentions go to pot.

'Oh don't be such a silly old fart,' I say. 'I may not be much of a gardener and I know the place is in a bit of a state. But I tell you what, I'm a jolly good mother and that's where my priorities are at the moment.'

And with that I turn around and go indoors. I shall not be bullied!

*

I don't like cats. I never have, but that doesn't mean I would hurt one.

'Nick, Nick, there's a cat at the back door. Can it come in?'

I think for a moment then say to Elfie, 'No, just leave it.'

It is still there the next day so I pop round and ask Emmi if it is hers. She assures me that it is not; she has no idea whose it could possibly be and urges me not to feed it unless I want to keep it.

'Please can we give it some food? It looks so hungry,' pleads Dan.

'No,' I say, and repeat what Emmi had told me.

'But I've always wanted a cat,' he whines.

'We've enough animals. No!'

When I come back from hanging out the washing, the boys are huddled around the cat feeding it bits of cold chicken; well, their tea as it happens.

'Now it won't ever want to leave us, will it?' says Dan, just as Elfie emerges from the kitchen with a bowl of milk and puts it down in front of the cat.

'What shall we call him?' they ask in unison.

Ever the optimist, I say, 'Let's just call him Puss until his real owners turn up to claim him back.'

But they never do.

Elfie and Dan are to start their new school this week. The nearest primary for us is three villages away so there is huge excitement – the children will go on the bus!

'Tell you what,' I say to them the day before, 'I think we should do a recce. Come on, let's see if we can find out where to catch it.'

As we walk down the road I notice a tall, slim girl with waist-length hair. Despite looking far too young to be a mother, she is pushing a baby in a pram with a toddler talking animatedly by her side.

She stops and holds out her hand. 'Hi,' she says with a broad smile. 'I'm Maggie, and you must be the newcomers.'

'Hallo, yes, I'm Nicky,' I say, shaking her hand. 'You don't happen to know where the school bus stops do you?'

'I'm not too sure, Sophie's not actually at school yet. She's only three. But I have a feeling it stops outside the church. Tell you what, why don't we walk down that way. We're bound to pass someone who knows,' she says.

'That would be great,' I say, 'if you're sure you don't mind.'

'It's no trouble, I'd enjoy the company. You know how isolating it can be with babies. So how old are your children?' Maggie continues, as we set off towards the church.

Before I have a chance to answer, the April child announces proudly 'I'm ten.'

I notice Maggie giving him a very old-fashioned look. She turns sympathetically toward me with a worried expression on her face. 'Ten?'

I shake my head and laugh, 'Goodness no, he's hardly three but he likes to think he's older. This is Elfie, she's eight, and Dan is six.'

Maggie looks relieved that my youngest is not as unusual as she first thought. 'He always pretends to be grown up. I've promised them a telly when they're older, and he thinks it'll speed things up a bit,' I explain. 'I take it you live in the village?'

'Yes, back there,' she says, pointing to a house almost next to the museum. It used to belong to my husband Mick's grandmother. We moved here about a year ago just before James was born.'

As we continue our walk, Maggie points out various cottages and tells me snippets about their inhabitants. She is obviously a gentle soul and would struggle to say anything derogatory about anyone. In the kindest way she explains a little about village politics and the goings on. Just before we reach the church, there is a high bank with a hawthorn hedge running along the top.

'You can't see it,' she says pointing, 'but George and Daisy live here. Behind there is the best vegetable garden I've ever seen.' As she speaks, a grey-haired head appears above the hedge and grins down at us.

'Afternoon George,' shouts Maggie. 'Just the person we're looking for. This is Nicky, and we want to know where the school bus stops in the morning and what time.'

George gives us a toothless grin and waves his arm in the direction of the lynch gate. 'Over there, just by the church yard,' he says. 'You can even shelter under the little porch if it rains. Reckon it comes about eight o'clock.'

Then to my horror he looks at me and says, 'So you're the unmarried mother with the three ruffians that's moved into the Goddards' old place. Whatever is the village coming to?'

I thank him and we turn for home. But somehow, with that chance remark, I felt the colour drain from my face as surely as the light was draining from the day.

'Oh Maggie,' I say, when we are out of hearing. 'Oh Maggie, is that what the village thinks?'

'I wouldn't take any notice of him. These village folk have nothing better to do than gossip.'

At our front gate I say goodbye to our new friends. But despite the promise to meet up again soon, as I walk the children down the path, my heart feels like a stone.

Just when I want to shut out the world, there is a knock at the door. The curtains are drawn so whoever it is can't see in. I decide to ignore it and get on with making supper. But the door opens and in walks a middle-aged woman with an open, friendly face. She is carrying a huge box of fresh vegetables. 'Hello,' she says with a ready smile, putting the box down on the table. 'I'm Katherine. I've just been dismantling all the harvest bits in the church and I thought these might be of use. I know Jean was keen on her flowers but she could never be bothered with a vegetable garden.'

'Gosh, thank you so much,' I said immediately, warming to this friendly soul. 'Would you like a cup of tea?'

'I won't now, I've still got lots of deliveries to do, but another time. Oh, and by the way, I notice you've a horse in the garden.'

Here we go, I think. 'Yes?' I say tentatively.

'Well, have you met Sidney yet? He keeps ponies up at the monastery. I think you'll like him.'

I could have hugged her.

Chapter 10

Our First Christmas

I put the phone down on my sister. She is anxious that we spend Christmas with her and her family. I know she means well; she has been unbelievably kind through all of this but I am resolute.

Christmas is always such an emotive time of the year. I have this abiding feeling that if I can face our first Christmas without Ben, not just face it but get through it with a degree of enjoyment, then I am well on my way to fulfilling my goal: to reach a happiness of sorts that is not dependent on a man.

I have decided we shall decorate the house only with greenery, either from the forest or our garden. Yes, we shall have fairy lights and tree decorations but everything else will be natural. No golds or silvers or glitters but a real proper evergreen affair.

I harness up the donkey while the children put on their boots and muffle up. I so want to make this Christmas memorable. As we set off towards the forest, I beam up a personal request for snow. For the moment though, we have to content ourselves with a cold, crisp sunny sort of a day.

I love the quiet that envelopes us in the middle of the pine woods; it's like another world, a secret world. A tiny coal tit darts along a branch and watches as I tie the donkey to a fallen tree.

'Now boys,' I say, giving them each a basket. 'I want you to pick up fir cones – as many as you can manage. Elfie and I are going to find a tree.'

It doesn't take us long; the strong autumn winds have brought down some huge branches of Scots pine so we are spoilt for choice. With their bluey-green needles and tightly closed cones we decide they would make the perfect Christmas tree. I let the Elf choose the piece she likes best, then I saw it off and drag it back to the cart.

The boys are happily engaged in pelting each other with cones but they have gathered masses, enough to decorate the house and still have lots to burn on the fire.

We all huddle together on the cart amongst our booty with the heady smell of pine wood filling our nostrils. Rose has her ears pricked up and breaks into a gentle trot.

'Come on you lot, time for a song. I have a feeling this Christmas is going to be alright.'

And now I wonder if being my usual stubborn self, I have done the right thing. Would the children be happier surrounded by cousins? Also it's the first Christmas without my father – perhaps I should be there for Mum. It's too late, though: I must stick to my plan.

And then the phone rings. I hesitate to answer it at first, fearing it might be the children's father who we anticipate a call from at any minute. I take a deep breath to compose myself before picking up the receiver.

'Hallo,' says an unfamiliar voice, 'it's the churchwarden here. I was wondering if you and the children might like to decorate the crib in the church. Judy's gone down with the flu.'

My immediate reaction is to say 'no'. I still have so much to do. I haven't even started to decorate our tree, let alone our own crib.

The churchwarden pre-empts my reply with, 'Oh please, I'd be so grateful.'

'Okay, of course we will,' I say. 'What do I need to bring?'

'Everything's on the pew, and I've put the stable up, but if you've got some hay or straw that would be marvellous. Oh, thank you so much,' says a relieved voice, then rings off.

Why can't I ever just say 'no'? I'm always pushed into things and I've got enough on my own plate.

After a hurried breakfast I persuade the children to get dressed while I collect a bag of hay and some fir cones.

'Come on you lot, get your coats on, it looks like we might get some snow,' I say, pushing Joe's feet into his wellies.

Some moments in life are as near to perfect as they can be. For me they are always when I least expect them and invariably involve the elements. Another component, and yes, I have tried to analyse them, is that they can never ever be orchestrated. As if on cue, snow is beginning to fall as we make our way towards the church. The sky is heavy and large flakes float down on the still air.

Inside the church, the organist is practising some carols while the village worthies go about their flower arrangements. I notice Katherine decorating the rood screen with great swathes of holly and ivy and make a mental note to ask her if she might show me how to make them one day.

The little stable stands in the quiet corner usually reserved for reading. Beside it is a big cardboard box containing all the nativity figures. I set Joe to unwrapping them while Elfie and Dan cover the crib floor with hay. At first it looks quite forlorn, but gradually the figures emerge: a camel here, an ox there, then Mary, Joseph – all take their place in this age-old story. When it is nearly finished, Joe unwraps the manger, but we can't find Jesus anywhere. We leave Dan rummaging through the bottom of the box while Joe and I go in search of the vicar.

'Do you know where Jesus has got to?' asks Joe. 'He's not in the box.'

'Well he hasn't actually been born yet,' replies the vicar, winking at me.

'But I know where he is, and if you all come to Midnight Mass tonight, I think we might find him. Why don't you come and see for yourself?'

By the time we bid our farewells, the church has taken on a truly joyful look. Garlands of greenery festoon the windows while a huge Christmas tree fills the back of the church. It is a timeless scene: a village church being adorned for the great Christian festival, and all by gentle country folk.

Outside the snow is coming down fast. As we walk along the path, the heavy silence is pierced by the strains of the organ playing 'Good Christian Men Rejoice'.

Joe slips his hand into mine while the older two rush ahead laughing and tumbling on the freshly fallen snow.

'Does the vicar really know where Jesus is?' he asks.

With the cosy glow of light from its leaded windows, our little cottage with its blanket of snow resembles a Victorian Christmas card. Puss is sitting in the window, looking out, awaiting our return. It could have been choreographed.

As we walk up the garden path I know I have made the right decision; this is going to be a magical Christmas.

Part Two

Lifting the Lid

Chapter 11

Siblings

Despite being fashioned from exactly the same cake mix, my sister and I are dramatically different. Now it may have been the shape of the tin that was altered or perhaps, quite simply, someone changed the oven temperature. But side by side on the cooling rack we could never be confused: she's the fairy and I'm the fruit.

✿ There is a story that has been retold endlessly in our family; I don't recall how old we were, but certainly not very. It was New Year's Eve and we were going to stay with a stuffy old aunt, a huge adventure in those days. Whatever possessed our usually domineering, interfering mother to allow us to pack our own suitcases, unaided, baffles me. I had never packed before, and nor do I recall ever having been anywhere that necessitated packing; the criteria was completely new to me. And it would appear my sister was also unfamiliar with its conventions. But we managed and no one checked.

Our cases were already upstairs when we were shown into the little double room.

My mother waltzed in looking her usual glamorous self and told Terry and me to bathe and put our frocks on for supper. It was at eight o'clock sharp and Aunt B was a stickler for time.

'What frock do you mean?' I asked. 'I haven't brought a frock.'

'Don't be so silly. Of course you've brought one,' continued Mum.

I shrugged my shoulders and glanced towards my sister.

'But what's in there?' asked Mum, walking over and peering into my case. It was full of endless little bundles of paper. She picked one of them up and began to unwrap it and there to her surprise was a small china horse. She placed it on a table and took out another bundle. I knew what it was, but I watched her remove the paper and put another little white horse beside the first.

Then she rummaged a bit more. 'There are no clothes in here at all. Where's your wash bag? Good grief,' she continued, 'your case is full of china horses. Is that all you've brought?'

'Terry, do you have a frock Nicky can wear?' asked my mother, walking towards my sister's case. Terry smiled nervously, but at least she had the good grace to look a little sheepish.

Mum pulled out a frilly petticoat. 'Well, I suppose that's better than ornaments,' she said. Then she pulled out another . . . frilly petticoat.

'Well, where's the frock to go over them?'

'I haven't brought a frock. I've just brought all my petticoats,' said Terry. 'I love them so much I didn't want to leave them behind.'

I didn't dislike my sister; I hardly even registered that I had one. While she was kind, decorative and malleable, I was the complete opposite; all that she wasn't. I'm sure it wasn't deliberate on my part.

It's the same with my own children; the same cake mix but such individual characters. I believe now that we arrive with our very own programming. Joe was such an unbelievably placid baby I quite thought there must be something wrong with him; so much so I called the doctor. After extensive prodding, measuring and checking all his spark plugs, the doctor turned to me and said with a big grin on his face, 'Enjoy him. You've got a good baby at last!'

I feel that, like the lean and the fat years, children go through good and bad patches and it really has very little to do with parental influence. Hence a trying toddler may well metamorphose into a truly easy teenager.

Gender makes a difference too. Interestingly, some differences became obvious at a very early age. I remember when the older two were little, before Joe arrived on the scene. They were playing happily in the sandpit while I did a spot of weeding. A ladybird landed on my arm and I called out to the Elf to come and look at it. She ran over to see what I had in my outstretched hand.

'Oh!' she said, 'isn't it beautiful. It's even lovelier than the one in my book.'

'Do you remember the poem, darling,' I said. 'Ladybird, ladybird fly away home . . . ?'

'Oh, I love it, can I keep it? I'll make it a little home in a matchbox.'

'No, darling, that wouldn't be fair.'

'Oh please . . . I could put some cotton wool in and make it so cosy.'

'I'm sure you would, and it's a lovely thought, but it is much better to simply enjoy looking at them, study them, then let them go. I tell you what, why don't we start a nature scrapbook. You can draw things you find and write down where you found them. Perhaps press some flowers and stick in bird feathers . . .'

As we were planning our project, Dan arrived and pushed himself between our legs to get a better view of whatever was capturing our attention.

'Look Danny,' said Elfie. 'A ladybird . . .'

And before she could say any more, Dan whacked my hand from beneath, the ladybird fell to the ground whereupon my three-year-old son trod on it.

'Dan kill it,' he said with a satisfied grin.

The Elf burst into tears but not before aiming a kick at her little brother and pulling his hair. He in turn, completely bemused, began flailing out at her. I intervened and sent Dan to his room to await a punishment that would fit the crime, although I wasn't actually convinced that I should punish him. Perhaps a good talking to would be more in order. I racked my brains for an Aesop's fable or a fairy tale that might be an allegory of what I had just witnessed.

So here are two siblings who, despite gender, had received identical instructions as to the complexities of life. What, I wonder, led them to display such polarity in their reaction to a harmless little beetle?

That may well have been the first time I uttered the words, 'Go to your room, Dan', but it has, over the intervening years, become a family refrain, in use almost every day. I notice bruises on Joe's legs, for instance. 'Darling, whatever are those?' I ask. 'They look quite nasty.' He feigns ignorance as to how he came by them. But there is a great deal that I can see from my vantage point at the kitchen window. The next evening I see Dan filling his pockets with crab apples. Unaware of my eye on him, he proceeds to pelt them at his younger brother. I also note he's a jolly good shot, but that's not really the point. Poor little Joe is tearing about trying to avoid another when I open the window and yell, 'Dan . . . go to your . . .' I hardly need to finish the sentence.

When I mention it the next morning and tell him not to be so beastly, his explanation is that the crab apples are the most perfect weight for throwing. 'I've tried the cooking apples but they're a bit too big,' he admits.

'Thank heavens for that,' I say, 'you could have knocked out the poor little chap.'

Girls too are not without their idiosyncrasies. Although not visible to the naked eye, I'm convinced we are surrounded by Barbie spores. Recently my daughter had a liberal sprinkling of them and now talks of little else.

Mum has kindly indulged this ghastly phase and sent her a Crystal Barbie complete with long golden tresses. I have to confess that, much as I love my daughter, I would find it difficult to execute such a purchase myself, so I am grateful to my mother.

The noise in the corridor is loud and coming closer.

'Nick, Nick!' cries my first-born as she screeches into the kitchen.

'Look what Dan's done,' she screams, while thrusting a doll in my face. 'He's cut all her hair off.'

And there before me is a bald-headed Barbie doll. I stifle a giggle while trying to placate my sobbing daughter.

'Go to your room Dan,' I say.

But for all the calamities, there are, mercifully, some

wonderful moments to lift the spirits. Even when things were at their very best between Ben and me, and there are some lovely memories, I always felt there was something missing. I would joke with him that he lacked a soul. I always promised to give him one for Christmas.

I looked the definition up: 'The part of the person that is not the body.'

When I first went to confirmation classes, there was much talk about our souls. My twelve-year-old self found the concept of something so intangible hard to grasp. The vicar asked us to imagine what they might look like, to picture our souls as we all sat about gazing at walls. Then to my horror he asked me to describe how I perceived my own. I replied that I saw it as large and pink. The rest of the class began to giggle, which of course started me off. Then before I knew it I was asked to leave the room as I was quite obviously too immature and not taking the preparation for my confirmation seriously enough. I still feel it was very unjust; I genuinely did not understand.

Dan's room is always a muddle; like that of most children his age. Apart from a weekly trawling for clothes to wash and changing his bed, I have always taken the view that it was his domain and as such, sacrosanct. I pop in to make sure he is up and half ready for school when I notice the sole from one of his trainers pinned to the back of his door. 'What's that, darling?' I ask.

He smiles his big open smile. 'It's my soul.'

Against my better judgement, Mum has thought to send the children a television. As she had it addressed specifically to them, there is not a lot I can say or do about it. They are completely over the moon and I have to confess I'm secretly delighted as well. It sort of gets them out of my hair from time to time. Why didn't I think of it, instead of adopting such a superior attitude? It would have simplified much ages ago. Good old Mum.

Chapter 12

Schools

I visited the primary school the children are to attend prior to the move; my decision to do so was based not so much on choice but rather the lack of it. The school in our tiny hamlet, and likewise in many of our neighbouring villages, has closed down. The old schoolhouses, where generations of local children have learned, have been snapped up and silently await the weekender.

Despite the cursory nature of my initial once-over, I am delighted to discover the school is everything I could wish for the children. At the moment there are fewer than fifty pupils who are taught in three classes. It appears that a lot of the children are related and so there is a lovely, gentle family atmosphere. I am also taken by how much less competitive schooling seems these days.

One day I arrive early to collect the children and am invited to watch the end-of-week assembly. I step inside and hear the time-honoured hymn, a prayer and the usual fidgeting. All very familiar territory from my own childhood except for one very radical difference: no one gets reprimanded. The feedback is all praise: praise for reading, for being generally helpful, for watering the guinea pig, improving at maths.

I watch as a child from each class is awarded a small prize, not necessarily for being the best, but for trying hard and/or general improvement. The children positively glow and I remember some words on a poster at our health centre. *If children live with encouragement they learn confidence, praise they learn to appreciate, fairness they learn justice.* And I think back sadly to my own experience of such assemblies. I continually feigned some illness to avoid going to them in the knowledge that whatever good I might have done, some old bat would be sure to mention the one thing I'd done wrong. This resulted in the inevitable detention and public humiliation before the entire school.

So it is a great joy to see these little children glowing with pride and good humour.

'Now, someone forgot to feed the goldfish. He knows who and so do I, but we'll leave it at that. Next week he must remember his responsibilities.'

What would they have made of me on the day my pony Snowball was a bit off colour? Would they have been quite so lenient when they told me to remember my responsibilities?

🌿 I suppose I must have been about ten years old: I held the halter as Mr Mackenzie ran his hand down my beloved pony Snowball's neck, then over her entire body. It wasn't often we called the vet; after all, she was a sturdy little Connemara mare and, as such, pretty hardy. But the rash or heat bumps that I could feel under her coat when I groomed her worried me. Also, she had started to rub her mane and it was already bald in places.

'I don't think we've too much to worry about,' he said, patting her firmly on the rump. 'I think her blood's a bit heated. Cut down on the hard feed, especially oats, and give her a daily bran mash with a good couple of handfuls of flowers of sulphur. That should do the trick. You can get a packet at the chemist. She could do with losing a bit of weight too; you know these native ponies are good doers. Won't do to overfeed them. Phone me in a week's time if there's no improvement.'

With that, he jumped into his Land Rover and drove off.

The next morning as I biked to school I made a detour by way of the chemist and bought a large box of flowers of sulphur. I checked my watch and realised I would have to rush if I didn't want to get a detention for being late . . . again.

I arrived in the playground just as the bell was ringing. There was no time to change into my indoor shoes so I grabbed the box and ran as fast as I could towards the assembly hall. I lined up at the back with all the other Lower Thirds, frantically doing up my tie, while trying to flatten my hair and hoping no one would notice my shoes.

Standing next to me in assembly was a girl called Jane Walker. I didn't particularly like her, not least because she always had a bag of sweets for break. I would hover about her, fascinated by Milky Ways and sherbet dabs and all manner of things forbidden to me. Mostly I didn't like her because she would never swap any of these for say . . . an apple, despite my assuring her it would be so much nicer.

As everyone opened their hymnbooks for the first song, I began to read the writing on the box. I couldn't resist opening it and having a look at the bright yellow powder. I stuck my finger into it and gave it a lick. It was surprisingly dry and caught the back of my throat. I stifled a cough.

Jane looked down at the box. 'What've you got there?' she asked in her stupid whiney voice.

I placed my hand over the writing so as she couldn't read it.

'It's sherbet,' I said, 'a new kind that my aunt's just sent me.'

'Can I have some?' she asked, predictably.

Bit of a nerve really, I thought, given her stinginess where her own sweets were concerned. I must confess at this particular juncture I did hesitate, but only for a second. But I reasoned that as she was spotty and slightly overweight she might actually benefit from a dose of my newly acquired remedy.

'Hold out your hand,' I whispered.

She did as I said and I tipped a heap of sulphur into her palm.

Jane raised her hand to her opened mouth and I watched her reptilian tongue dart out and scoop up a great dollop. Just as I was registering the disgust on her face, Lardy, our headmistress, strode into the hall. In her panic, Jane stuffed the remaining powder into her mouth. Immediately the piano struck up, we straightened our backs, held our heads high and began to sing.

Well, all except Jane that is, who began to splutter.

As we all belted out the morning hymn, Jane's spluttering was gaining in momentum. It became a bit manic and then to my alarm sounded dreadfully like a choking noise.

I glanced at her and continued singing as loud as I possibly could.

By now we were attracting a deal of attention, not least from our form teacher, Miss Bevan.

Gallantly I patted Jane on the back, but to no avail. To my horror she began to go puce in the face. Bev stepped forward and raised her hand. The piano stopped and the hall fell silent. All eyes turned towards us.

'Water,' shouted someone. 'A glass of water, that should do it.'

'Get her to the San. Quickly!' said another.

While we were all huddled about this contorted being, Lardy came striding along the hall with her gown billowing out behind her. The serried ranks of girls parted like the proverbial waves as she bore down on us.

'Get up, Jane,' she said. 'Get up! You are making a complete exhibition of yourself. Tell me child, what is going on. Goodness! Whatever is that substance around your mouth?'

'Please Miss,' gasped Jane , in between splutters. 'It's sherbet, Nicky gave me it.'

'Is this true?' The old harridan turned and glared at me.

I smiled inanely and nodded.

'What's this?' she said, snatching the box from my hand. 'This isn't sherbet it's . . . it's flowers of sulphur. What are you doing with it . . . and in school?'

Mercifully, Jane's choking lessened.

'Miss Bevan, I want you to take Jane and this box down to the San. Tell Matron what has happened. As for you,' Lardy said glaring down at me, 'go and wait in my study – immediately.'

'Girls,' she continued, 'we shall sing what remains of the hymn.' She waved to Miss Taylor at the piano and once more the hall was filled with children singing.

I felt all eyes on me as I left the assembly hall and made my solitary walk down familiar corridors. Endless reproductions of classical Greek gods and goddesses stared down disapprovingly from their pillars, compounding my humiliation.

Outside Lardy's study I stood and waited. Oh god! I hope it's not another detention, especially this afternoon. There couldn't be many more Shakespeare speeches to learn, I consoled myself. I made a mental note not to look too concerned. I knew already, oh how I knew, what a bully the old bat could be. How she delighted in meting out punishment.

'There you are, child – follow me.' Lardy opened the door and ushered me in. I stood to attention in front of her desk and watched as she settled her ample self into a chair on the other side.

Her back was to the window, or I should say windows; three large bay windows through which you could see directly over the playing field. Many a time Lardy would stand staring out at us, watching our every move.

As luck would have it, my class had games for the first lesson and as I looked out, to my horror, some of my classmates were already lining up outside the window, staring in and pulling faces, sticking out tongues and generally gesticulating so as to make me laugh. I tried to keep a straight face. I succeeded until Maureen Boyd did a handstand and I began to snigger.

'This is not a laughing matter, Nicola. How dare you take this so lightly,' said Lardy. 'And just look at the state of you. Why, you haven't even changed your shoes. Are you listening to me? What's so amusing?' she turned just in time to catch a glimpse of Maureen's bottom.

'That's it; I've had enough of you and your gang. You are without doubt the worst Lower Third this school has ever known. But firstly where did you obtain the flowers of sulphur and what were you doing with it in school?'

I explained as honestly as I could.

'But what on earth induced you to give some to a fellow pupil?'

I thought for a moment. I felt unable to explain my dislike of Jane and the fact she always had sweets that I was denied. I couldn't own up to petty jealousies.

Instead I blurted out, 'For a laugh.'

'For a laugh. For a laugh? Do you realise you could have killed her? For a laugh.'

'I didn't mean to harm her, she thought it was sherbet. The vet said it was good for spots and Jane's got plenty of those.'

'Don't be insolent. Frankly, Nicola, this is the last straw. As far as I am concerned, you are guilty of attempting to poison a fellow pupil.'

'But please,' I tried to reason. 'Surely if it's alright for Snowball, it couldn't kill someone. I knew it wasn't poison. That's not fair.'

'Life is not always fair as you will no doubt learn. Think yourself lucky that I shall not involve the police. But this is an end to it. I shall phone your mother and tell her to collect you immediately. YOU ARE EXPELLED!'

While I was secretly delighted to be leaving that particular school, I was filled with remorse in later years. If I choose to reflect on such a cavalier attitude towards a fellow pupil, it is in the knowledge that the only casualty was my reputation.

꽃 꽃 꽃

Over the years I have learnt to approach parents' evenings with caution. The spectacle of married couples taking a shared interest in their offspring's schooling only serves to remind me of my solitary state. It is a time when I particularly miss the presence of the children's father. Not simply for moral support; I should so love him to be here to delight in their achievements.

There are also times when I need convincing that the unsolicited praise heaped on one or other of my children is not a mighty wind-up from the teacher.

One such evening I am in the school hall, mingling and exchanging niceties with other parents as we await our allotted time. Around the walls hang an assortment of the children's work, poems, pictures and little stories, and we all smile proudly at each other as we search for our own youngsters' handiwork.

As I read my way around the room searching for a familiar name, I am aware of a group of mums standing by a piece of work. I stop beside them and recognise my daughter's name. They stand back so I can get a better view to read.

BEING TOLD OFF

My mum is sometimes horrible to me. She shouts at me and she gets the horse whip out and whips me till I am red and if we tell a lie and she finds out my mum will say you disobedient little girl to not own up and the nice thing about her is when we tell the truth she is nice to us.

Elfina Hodgkinson

Now, we were brought up to 'never complain and never explain'. Not that I have necessarily always heeded such advice. But I do feel a little explanation is in order here. To enlarge on the above: it's true I do own a whip. It sits in a basket by the kitchen door along with walking sticks and rounders bats. I admit there have been times when I have had occasion to grasp it in my right hand and wave it threateningly in the direction of wayward children, and my goodness, it works a treat. But I can honestly say I have never actually used it on a child.

After that I approach Dan's contribution with a degree of caution:

It was a dark and stormy night. I was alone in the house.
My mum was down at the pub as usual . . .

Somehow I lack the heart to finish reading it, let alone justify it to anyone who might care to listen. But hey! The joy of the children owes much to their unpredictability, or so I keep trying to convince myself. I am emptying Dan's trouser pockets before popping them in the wash one night when I find a crumpled up note. 'Oh that's from my girlfriend,' he says, all seven years of him. His reading is not really up to speed so he asks me what the note said.

'I love you!' I read out to him.

'Ugh, how soppy,' he exclaims. 'She wets her pants, even when she's playing.'

But however naughty or spirited they may be at home, there are times when they surpass themselves at school. Driving home from the school one winter's afternoon, Dan announces proudly: 'I won this year's prize for endeavour.'

'Darling, how wonderful, is that for your class? Or your year?'

'Neither, it's for the whole school,' he replies excitedly.

'Well I think that's terrific! You must think up something you'd like as a treat.'

We are just turning into the cottage, it is pitch-dark by now. Suddenly his voice pipes up again.

'Nick . . . What does "endeavour" mean?'

And his French is coming along apace: I noticed in his homework recently . . . 'Mon chat s'appell Pooosie.'

I so long to share the joy I feel at such moments. I long to tell someone. But not just anyone, preferably his father.

Chapter 13

Salad Days

I have mentioned it before: I was not the child my mother wanted. But nor indeed would she have been my first choice of mothers. That is not to say I didn't love her but I found it hard. I did, however, have a respect for her discipline and her direction.

Life was very black and white to her; there were no shades of grey. Given that my mother deems beauty imperative in everything she beholds, she has long since held the belief that overweight people should pay a fat tax. 'Paying a fat tax' is now a euphemism in our family for any one of us who has put on a few pounds.

She took a huge interest in every aspect of her appearance and as such was always a head-turner. Already blessed with natural good looks, she constantly strove to look immaculate, even when gardening or painting.

Painting has always been Mum's first love, and it remains so. When we were children she had a painting hut – studio – at the top of the garden in a little fenced area known as the washing green. Here the washing was hung out, always on a Monday. Life was regulated in those far-off days. Even when it rained there seemed to be washing there or on a wooden pulley in the washhouse.

Anyway the little painting hut was known as 'Glasgow'. As a child it never struck me as odd, but looking back I'm not so sure.

The reasoning behind such a baptism went thus: when her perceived domestic duties were 'seen to', Mum would escape to Glasgow to paint. If someone called – a friend or what have you – not wishing us to fib on her behalf, my sister and I were told to reply in all honesty: 'I'm sorry, she's gone to Glasgow for the day and I don't know when she'll be back.'

For someone of Mum's innate natural elegance, it must have been baffling in the extreme to have produced a daughter like me. Not only could I turn untidiness into an art form, but I was completely disinterested in appearances, both my own and others'. I fear she found it infuriating.

ø 'What's this?' I asked, carrying a white lacy dress into my mother's bedroom. 'I found it on my bed.'

My mother was seated at her dressing table staring at herself in a triptych mirror. She didn't turn around; simply spoke to my reflection. 'Oh darling, it's your frock for the party tonight.'

'But it's Terry's, and anyway I've got my old blue one. I'll be fine with that, really.'

'Well, you see, Terry has a new one,' she said to the mirror as she tilted her head this way and that to get a view from all angles. 'It arrived from Harrods today and I thought it would be rather fun if you wore this. I know you're fatter and not as tall, but I've let it out at the seams and with a nice pink sash around your waist no one will notice the length.' She dabbed some cream on her face and began to rub it in with some rather bizarre upward movements.

I grimaced. 'Pink? Yuk.'

'I wish you wouldn't pull faces. You know if the wind changes you'll stay like that.'

'I hate lace and anyway I'd rather wear something I'm comfortable in. It's alright for Terry, she's two years older, but I'll feel a complete idiot in that. It's so girly.'

'Darling, don't be silly, you're growing up now. You'll soon be fourteen and it's time you took a bit more interest in your appearance.'

'Like you and Terry you mean?'

'Yes, like your sister. Unlike you, she's always been a joy to dress up. Ever since she was a tiny little thing, she's always loved clothes. Mind you, she's so pretty she could wear a sack and still turn heads.'

'Is that why she's forever getting new things?'

'Partly darling, but then the youngest always gets hand-me-downs. You don't mind, do you?'

'Of course not,' I replied in all honesty. I didn't mind what I wore as long as it wasn't frilly, lacy, overtly girly or, worse, didn't involve petticoats. Come to think of it, this just about covered my sartorially aware sibling's entire wardrobe.

I was conscious of my sister's beauty. It was remarked upon with such frequency I couldn't not be. If perchance I was in hearing distance of yet another eulogy, my father would smile indulgently in my direction and say, 'Ah, but of course Nick's the funny one.' And so, as my repertoire of stories burgeoned, I gradually assumed the role of family joker.

I digress . . . back to the evening.

'Darling, you must have a bath. Terry can have the first one, but tell her to leave the water in. Oh and do remember to wash your face . . . I think you should put on a little make-up tonight.'

'Absolutely not! That frock's one thing but I'm not wearing slap.'

My mother turned away from the looking-glass and stood up. She walked towards me with outstretched hands. 'You're like a little russet apple,' she said as she gently pinched my cheeks. 'You have such a lovely rosy complexion, but I do think a tiny bit of foundation might soften it a bit.'

Despite my feeling like something off the Christmas tree, the evening was going surprisingly well. We were seated around a large table, relaxing between dances, when we were joined by some very stuffy friends of my parents.

After the usual introductions, the woman leant towards my mother and I overheard her saying, 'Terry seems more beautiful every time I see her. She looks enchanting in that frock.'

'Thank you, Freda, she does look lovely,' said my mother, glowing with pride. And then almost in a whisper, 'I do wish we could say the same for Nicky. There are times when I quite despair of her.'

'Tell you what,' said my father. 'Why doesn't Nick tell us a story?'

I suggested singing *I Know an Old Lady Who Swallowed a Fly*, but was promptly met with groans of, 'Oh no, not again,' from my sister. 'Can't we have something new?'

I thought for a moment. 'I know,' I said. 'I heard this joke at the stables today. I didn't get the ending but everyone laughed so it must be good.'

'That will be fine,' said my father.

'There was this honeymoon couple and they were staying in a country pub,' I began. 'Every day the landlord took meals up to their room and left the tray outside the door, but the meals remained untouched. After three or four days he was getting a bit worried so he knocked on the door and called to them that as they hadn't eaten anything, was everything alright?'

I paused for a moment.

'Go on,' said my father winking at me.

'They answered back that they were fine and not to worry as they were living on the fruits of love. "That's all very well," shouted the landlord, "but would you please stop throwing the skins out of the window".'

I glanced around the table, anxious to gauge the reaction.

From the stunned silence I thought perhaps they didn't get the ending either.

Then my sister began to giggle nervously. 'I can't believe you've said that,' she whispered.

'Said what?' I replied.

'That joke. It's so rude.'

'Is it?' I said. 'I told you I didn't get it. I was hoping some-one would explain.'

I watched as my father began to laugh and took a hanky from his pocket to dab his eyes. Not so my mother, she remained po-faced . . . glaring at me. Her friends seemed unsure of how to react. Freda smiled nervously in my direction.

My mother broke the silence. 'Nicky, will you fetch your coat and go straight to the car?'

'Why? Whatever for?'

'You know jolly well what for. Just do as I say. NOW!'

Chapter 14

Star Wars

A recurring worry I have is: as I was such a naughty child, how do I have the audacity to take the moral high ground with my own children? I do so long to be the kind of mother my children want. But then, as they have no expectation of childhood, it will only be with time I'll know if I got it right.

One of the necessary evils of rearing children is that of discipline. All too often the parent who bears the larger part of the domestic chores so essential to family life – relentless meals, washing etc – also has the unsavoury task of tackling eating habits, bad language and general conduct unbecoming. It's most unfair. The very repetition of everyday nagging does nothing to enhance harmony; in fact, it can so readily chip away at the very foundations you are trying to build upon. It may also eclipse all the fun you can have with lively, if somewhat rebellious, youngsters.

It is made worse for the single parent if the other half is given to rocking up at weekends with endless treats.

My solution to this problem is to turn it into a game: the old 'spoonful of sugar' touch. Very simple but effective, it does make for a lighter hearted approach to the problem. It has evolved in our household, with many variations thereof, to become known as:

Star Wars
A game for any number of players
Object of the game: harmony in the household

How to play
All you will need is a piece of silicone paper/mirror or Perspex and a packet of sticky stars.

A list is drawn up of all the members of the household. The inclusion of the cat/dog/goldfish does not necessarily demean the game. Indeed, it may even enhance it. Enter each contestant's name at the top of the paper and stick five stars under each.

Object of the game
To end the week with more stars than anyone else!

Rules
Stars are awarded for voluntary acts of helpfulness, thoughtfulness, eating up what's put in front of you rather than the chocolate cake that has just been made for Granny's birthday. Homework or music practice completed without reminding, or generally anything you deem is an effort on that individual child's part.

It varies enormously from child to child, household to household. Joe gets one each time he gets his shoes on the correct feet. For the others, this would be folly. An unsolicited thank-you letter merits two stars.

The list is legion. Pancakes for breakfast are my big earner.

You may not bargain: 'If I wash up/wash the car/wash the hamster, can I have a star?'

'No.'

Stars are removed for winding up a sibling, or anybody else, rudeness, getting ketchup all over the dog, or bathing the hamster.

I too play the game and lose stars for bad language and stubbing cigarettes out on my plate: two the other day for telling a white lie on the telephone. As yet I have never won. This pleases the children enormously as they see that I also have to strive. It's important that the children feel a degree of control over their lives and it helps if they too can reward or remove stars with equal facility.

The prize

Whatever you or they deem worthwhile. I find £1 still goes a long way in this household. I know an endearing family where a tube of Smarties is enough of an incentive to make five unspoilt youngsters excel; it's entirely up to the individual family. If I ever do win, it will be a cup of tea in bed.

Prize giving

Friday night is our chosen time. In a frenzy of anticipation the children await the announcements. Whoever the winner, it is an auspicious moment to put in a general word on their individual behaviour. Beware, they too may choose to comment on yours.

The prize is presented amidst a round of applause and a

new chart begun; a new week, a new beginning. And you may just be pleasantly surprised with the offers of help with the washing-up.

But it's just struck me – I have no good habits . . . well, perhaps cleaning my teeth and writing thank-you letters. Apart from that, smoking, drinking, time wasting . . . the list of my bad habits is endless. I wonder if birds and wild animals acquire bad habits. Certainly domesticated animals do; perhaps it's their proximity to humans. I must give that some more thought.

And when does a habit become bad? When it annoys yourself or someone else?

I have seen all the *Star Wars* movies, whether or not I wanted to. In the absence of any other adult male recipient of my affection, I have to confess to becoming a bit of a Harrison Ford fan. I even covet the little *Star Wars* figure of him as Han Solo. Dan knows this and finds it highly amusing. I am washing up when he runs into the kitchen. He comes up to me with both of his hands behind his back.

'Which hand do you want?' he asks with a grin.

'What's this darling, what have you got behind your back?'

'I'm not telling you, come on, which hand . . . choose.'

I point to his left.

He unclenches his fist to reveal the head of Han Solo.

'What's in the other,' I muse.

He opens his other hand very slowly, and there in the palm was Han Solo's body.

He bursts out laughing. 'I trod on him, look he's broken. Now which bit do you want? Be honest: you can have his head or his body.'

I think for a moment, and then lie: 'Oh darling, I'd love his head. Thank you so much,' I say, popping him on the shelf above the kitchen sink.

So for the time being I content myself with a tiny plastic head of a Hollywood movie star while secretly yearning for his body.

Chapter 15

Cycling

There are times when I really wish the children's father was here with us to share, not just the grotty bits, but the joy. At a picnic on the beach, I watch other families with fathers: fathers who play ball, fathers who take the older children into the sea and teach them to swim. I sit in my usual state of vacillation. The Elf and Dan want to go into the water but as yet don't swim very well. The tide on this coast is strong. I deliberate. Do I, can I, leave the April child crawling about unattended while I give swimming lessons to the older two? I decide to take Joe with me but that leaves me with no arms to demonstrate the breast stroke. I put him down at the water's edge in the vain hope that clapping his hand on its surface will amuse him for long enough, and thus enable me to give the others a sporting chance. It's no use and as ever we all end up doing not very much.

It's the same when I take them to public loos. I'm fine taking my daughter into the ladies, even a male toddler; that's okay. But what do you do with a six-year-old boy? I am loath to let my little sprout wander into the gents on his own, but nor can I really follow him in, so inevitably he joins us in the ladies. I wonder if I am already beginning to confuse him.

He shouts from the next door cubicle, 'Nick, Nick, What does dopsal mean?'

I shout back that I haven't a clue what he's talking about.

'It's written on a tin in here,' he replies.

I glance down at the tin on our floor and read 'Sanitary Disposal'. And as ever I am evasive and change the subject as we wash our hands.

Today is overcast, slightly windy and dull. I could say, a bit like me. I must try to snap out of it. The April child has gone to play with Maggie's children, Sophie and James, so I shall take the older two for a good blustery bike ride. That should do the trick.

Halfway along the Heritage Coast is a small sprawling village by the name of Walberswick. It is a typical bucket-and-spade holiday spot, with the added attraction of crab fishing. Part of the charm of this particular stretch of coastline is the absence of a coastal road. To reach many of its quirky little villages and towns necessitates leaving the A12 and driving some miles eastwards. Conservation groups such as the Suffolk Wildlife and English Heritage now own great swathes of land. Desolate heathland, gorse and marshes all lend a feeling of adventure to our journey, as if we are discovering somewhere for the very first time.

The distance, as the clichéd crow flies, between Dunwich and Walberswick is about a mile, but the children and I have opted to bike what will be about five miles. Cycling around this part of Suffolk is great; not only is it very flat but there are miles of 'off road' tracks. This, to my six- and eight-year-old, is an awfully big adventure.

The first leg of our journey takes us through Dunwich Forest. While giving the impression of having been around for centuries, it was, I am told, only planted in the 1930s. Closer inspection does confirm the abundance of soft wood trees, and as such the forest is singularly devoid of interesting flora and fauna. What little of the latter it may have had appears to be flattened on the road, to Dan's delight.

At the Five Fingers crossroads, on the Westleton to Blythburgh road, we take a sharp right onto a very bumpy un-made track. Huge potholes filled with water from last night's storm, and the gnarled roots of ancient trees, add diversion to our expedition. The children are in their element riding through puddles and getting soaked. On we bike, on through the reed beds, where we stop and listen out for the ever-elusive bittern . . . but have no luck. However, we do have a wonderful sighting of another bird that's almost extinct, but not quite, thanks to the RSPB: the marsh harrier. We watch in awe as, high above us, it courses up and down the reeds searching for small mammals. Dan suggests, without a hint of irony, that it should have a look on the forest road. I try to explain carrion to him as best I can.

The last stage of our adventure is downhill all the way, negating a need to pedal. With the sea air rushing through our hair and the heady scent of gorse in full bloom filling our nostrils, we arrive exhilarated.

Wide-open skies and salt marshes abound. Immediately you can see why this tiny village, tucked away on the east coast, became a haven for an artistic movement in the nineteenth century. The light is sensational.

We eat a leisurely lunch in the pub garden. Marsh samphire, gathered this morning from the back of the beach and drip-ping in butter, is washed down with a pint of local Adnams ale, brewed only yards away, across the River Blythe in Southwold. The children opt for some deliciously refreshing homemade lemonade.

And now we are off to crab fish! We wander down to the very bridge captured by Wilson Steer all those years ago. Here the children lie on their tummies dangling old fish heads tied to pieces of string into murky-looking water. They wait good-naturedly for small crabs to feast on their bait. The trick, it seems, is to be very still. Slowly and very carefully, they haul the line out of the water and net the unsuspecting crab into a bucket of water. This requires a degree of skill not given to many and at times the air is blue with expletives. But I console myself by thinking the children are learning one of life's great lessons, to be patient. I must add that all the crabs are tipped back onto the water's edge at the end of a session. It is an innocent pursuit and a rite of passage to this, the quaintest of English villages.

And it is, for now, still special. Where else, pray, can grown men sport T-shirts boasting 'I Caught Crabs in Walberswick'?

On our leisurely bike ride home, we notice the prevalence of yellow flowers. Colours of the months have always fascinated me. It suddenly dawns on me, the flowers' need for such disarming brightness on dull days: to be pollinated before they wither and die. What a completely wonderful day. We've all loved it. Despite my inherent nagging inadequacies about parenting, it has been magical and hopefully will serve to remind me that I can do it.

It's late when we arrive home. We're starving hungry, exhausted and there is much to do. As I run a bath for the children, I am reminded of something my mother said to me when I got divorced. Contrary to what I believed would be the case, she gave me little sympathy; indeed she basically told me to pull myself together and get on with it. Whenever I have moaned about my lot she has constantly urged me to look on the bright side. When I complain about how lonely I am, she tries to make me see the positive: 'Think about it . . . You can stay out in the woods, or picnic till dark. If you had a husband who'd just come home from work you couldn't do that. You'd have to be there, making supper for him.' After a day like today I am beginning to see exactly what she means.

But again, this is the same mother who thought *Romeo and Juliet* was the most perfect love story; she would say they both died before they got to the disillusioned part . . . I mean, really.

Chapter 16

Settling In

The church and bus stop are at one end of our street. There is a pub and the sea at the other and Maggie and her family in between the two. I've decided our cottage is ideally situated.

After we have put the older two on the school bus, Joe and I have taken to going for long blustery walks along the beach with Maggie and her children. If we get there in time, we watch the fishermen land their catch and buy fresh Dover sole for tea. Joe becomes ever more fascinated by the different types of fish so we try to identify them. An unsuspecting lobster inadvertently caught up in the nets is a cause of huge excitement.

He and Sophie, being of a similar age, have struck up a firm friendship, resulting in a symbiosis of sorts for Maggie and me: already we look after each other's children on certain days of the week. There are times when others take them for siblings, so alike are they with their Titian-coloured hair.

'Why do your children call you by your Christian name?' asks Maggie. 'They never seem to say Mum.'

I think for a moment: it hadn't occurred to me before.

'I can only think they hear others calling me Nick. And given there's no father to call me Mum, I suppose it wouldn't occur to them.'

Gradually that daunting feeling of unease, of being the newcomers, is wearing off. After his initial caustic remark, George now waves to us over the hedge as we make our daily pilgrimage to and from the church. He has even invited Joe and me in and showed us his garden. It's quite obviously his pride and joy: an enormous vegetable patch surrounded by greenhouses, hen runs, little hutches with poorly chickens, orphaned ducklings, walnut trees, figs and lilac he had planted from seed. We talk mainly of poultry before he sends us on our way with a big smile, a bag of fresh peas and the promise of a duckling for Joe.

However, there are still moments when I want the earth to swallow me up!

I am on my way home from the bus stop when Emmi beckons to me over her gate.

'Come in,' she calls.

I undo the latch and walk towards her. She opens her outstretched hand to reveal an assortment of coins.

'I'm not sure what to say,' she says in a slightly affronted manner. 'Your Dan came round last night with his piggy bank.'

'Sorry,' I say, 'I don't understand.'

'I'm not sure I do either,' she continues, 'but he asked if he might come in, and then he emptied the contents onto the table and said, "Here, this is for you." I asked him what he was doing, and he said quite simply, "Nicky said you were poor so I thought I'd give you my money." He seemed so concerned I didn't like to refuse. So here, pop it back in his bank,' she says, tipping it into my hand.

I thank her and go home musing.

'Dan,' I say at tea-time, 'whatever made you take money round to Emmi?'

'Well, you said she was poor,' he replies.

'No, I didn't. It was really embarrassing.'

'You did. You definitely said "poor Emmi"'.

I rack my brains for a moment, then laugh.

'You sweet boy,' I say. 'You're right. I did say "poor Emmi", but it was only because her little dog had just died.'

But I can't always blame the children for embarrassing situations; I have to admit to the occasional own goal myself.

I am fed up with casual callers. I have hung a sign on the door saying PISS OFF I'M BUSY. Only dear Emmi has just come round; she is collecting for the Lifeboats and I notice her looking at it and turning away. I rush out into the garden and apologise profusely. It would have to be her that read it first. I have taken it down and decide to hide in the wagon when I want time to myself. I must think up a suitable name for it so the children don't have to lie on my behalf!

Mum has been staying all week. I can't make out if it is the pleasure of our company or maternal concern that brought her back; no matter, it is a great success. She arrives on Monday and leaves on Friday. Unlike the first unfortunate experience with the misunderstanding about the wagon, it all goes very well. I am delighted as I'd dreaded it so much. Of course there was the usual rushing about like a dervish, cleaning up and sticking flowers in every available jar, but it was all worth it.

I dedicate the whole week to entertaining her, and with a case of fizzy wine in the pantry and the children on their best behaviour, it couldn't have gone better. I keep waiting for her to turn on me, to find fault with something and lay into me.

But no, if she does feel like it, she certainly bites her tongue. It is a great weight off my mind, and hopefully will help when we go down to Devon for the summer.

So many people have strained relationships with their families, and it shouldn't be so. I find it desperately sad and it's something I dearly wish to comprehend before my own children leave home. I shall do everything in my power to avoid such a situation with my lot.

We are chatting in the kitchen when the Elf comes back from a ride. Her long blonde hair is dishevelled and her freckled face slightly flushed from the fresh air. As she leaves the room Mum says, 'Darling, would you mind, I'd really love to paint Elfina. She's still at that gloriously unselfconscious stage; but you know any minute now it will all change.'

'I'd love that, Mum, I really would. But I could take a photo.'

'I know,' she says, 'but I always think a portrait can capture the essence of a person in a way a photo never can.'

'Well I think it's a brilliant idea, thank you.'

Later, I stand quietly in the doorway. Mum is so engrossed in her painting she doesn't hear me.

The Elf is sitting on a raised chair with her gaze fixed toward the window. I'm delighted to see her hair is unbrushed and tumbles about her shoulders. She is wearing an open-necked shirt and there is still a youthful innocence about her.

I see all this on the canvas before me. But what Mum has also captured is something almost unperceivable to the naked eye: the merest hint of transition.

It's chucking it down with rain today, rare in these parts. It's the first time I can remember the children donning wellies and raincoats to walk to the bus and there is much complaining. It must be my Scottish childhood, but I adore the rain and such mornings. Feeling very nostalgic, I walk along the beach and then to the cliffs – it is heaven. Now whether this is the place to indulge such whims or a coming to terms with my lot, I don't know. It may even, dare I say it, be a direct result of Mum's visit. Whatever the cause, at last I feel very 'right' here.

Chapter 17

Home Sweet Home

Perhaps if I hadn't been so wilful, I may never have been expelled. And if I hadn't been expelled I may never have been sent away to boarding school . . . perhaps. I think, with hindsight, my poor mother found me very difficult to handle. Maybe it was the only way she could cope; but I do wish she hadn't lied.

🖋 She said it would do me good. I had grown wild; it was time I went to boarding school. And besides, homesickness is a horrible thing; it would be better if I got over it now, while I was still young. But that first journey, that first train away from everything I knew, spoilt it all.

I should have realised when she said 'the midnight sleeper'. I was bewitched, seduced by the excitement, others' enthusiasm. How was I to know as I watched her pack my trunk?

It was dark at the station. I remember feeling self-conscious in the horrid uniform, everything so new. My knees were cold and she gave me a hug. Not until I heard the first rumblings of the train did I sense fear. Like some fabulous creature of the night, it roared out of the dark, hissing and threatening.

Terrified, I wanted to turn and run, but instead she willingly gave me up to the gigantic beast. Paralysed with fear, I boarded the train and waited as the engine gathered strength. Motionless, I stared through the window at her beaming face. Powerless, I watched her waving arms. The next moment she was out of sight. I beseeched the monster to turn back but it would not listen. Relentlessly it thundered on into the night, carrying me away from everything I knew.

The train blanket smelt unfamiliar and I longed for my own bed and for her to tuck me in. As I wept silently into British Rail sheets, I could hear her saying it would be good for me.

As I remembered the last gallop along the beach, saying goodbye to the sea and the hills, that journey taught me to cry alone, little knowing it was only me who would change. Apart from my bedroom, that is . . .

I returned home from boarding school, ebullient about the prospect of endless summer days stretching into the horizon. After long months of institutionalised living, of sharing dormitories and almost everything else, the bliss of returning to my very own room complete with all its familiar muddle was overwhelming. The thought of it had sustained me through many a stark lonely night.

I ran towards my beloved bedroom, disregarding my mother's shouting from behind me. 'Darling, wait a minute . . . let me explain!'

But I didn't wait. Instead I threw open the door and stared in horror.

I let out a gasp; it must be some kind of joke. I closed the door thinking perhaps when I opened it again all would be well. This time I was more cautious. I stared in disbelief.

'Oh darling, I wish you'd given me time to explain,' said my mother, who had now caught up with me. 'Don't you think it's delightful? We really needed an extra bathroom, especially at this end of the house.'

'But where am I to sleep . . . where's my room . . . what's happened to all my stuff?'

'Come with me, darling. Please don't be upset. Mrs Wilson and I have made a room for you up on the top floor.'

'What do you mean the top floor? We don't have a top floor. You mean the loft, don't you?' I said, as I followed my mother along the corridor and up the old wooden staircase.

I had been in the attic before but only to help pack away Christmas decorations or school trunks; all I could remember was it was dark and very pokey, certainly not big enough for a bedroom.

And I was right. The ceiling was only just high enough for me to stand up straight in the middle, a width of a few feet. The rest of the walls sloped down to the floor. There was a little single bed tucked into a corner and one very small chest of drawers.

'Don't you think it's charming? Look, we've even had a window put in. It's so cosy.'

I looked around the cramped space. *Cosy* was a euphemism too far. 'Where are my china horses?' I asked. 'And my egg collection?'

'Oh darling, don't you think you're too old for all that kind of thing now?'

'What do you mean? Where are they?'

'It's not important. Come and look at the view.'

'Mum, what have you done with my desk?'

My mother stood on her toes and peered out of the window, feigning indifference to my pleas.

'Tell me what you've done with all my things. There were letters and stuff in the drawers, where are they? Why have you done this anyway?' I shouted at her.

'Please don't raise your voice, there's no need for it. I thought as you are so rarely here it would be nice to have a new bathroom.'

'Rarely here! Of course I'm rarely here! You sent me away to bloody school, that's why I'm rarely here . . . in case it didn't occur to you.'

'Nicky, will you please not shout at me.'

'Tell me what you've done with all my things. MY THINGS! You've got rid of them, haven't you?'

'It's not like that, let me explain. You can see there's no room for the desk, so I sold it. And Mrs Wilson's little girl really loved your china horses . . . so I . . .' she hesitated.

'So you gave them away! *I* really loved those horses; they were mine. You had no right to give them away. I've been collecting them for years. Most of them were presents . . . how dare you.'

'Don't talk to me like that, this is my house. If you can't be bothered to look after your things, then I can do with them as I choose. Your bedroom was constantly in a mess anyway; and it's always been an issue getting you to tidy it.'

'I can't believe you've done this,' I screamed, already too heavy-hearted to continue the row. In time-honoured fashion my mother had won and I knew there was no point in saying any more. Instead I ran for the stairs.

'Where are you going?' she shouted after me.

'I'm going to see Snowball. That's if you haven't turned the stables into a granny annex.'

'Darling, wait! I've something else to tell you . . .'

✎ ✎ ✎

Chapter 18

Old Friends

The Elf has always loved rabbits. Her very first pet was a white rabbit which, for reasons best known to herself, she named Ginger. But that was before we moved here. Her constant companion now is a black rabbit called Bun. And when I say constant, I mean it. She would take him to school if I let her. He sleeps in her bedroom and is almost, but not quite, house-trained. I would never credit a rabbit with much in the way of feelings but Bun has an abiding dislike of my oldest friend Docker. This he manifests in a rather shocking way. Well, once we have all stopped laughing, I feign shock. I could understand his reaction to her if she was not such an animal lover, but every time he comes into the sitting room and sees her sitting on the sofa he dashes towards her in top gear. He then jumps up at her, starts peeing all over her while doing a flying turn and runs off again. The first time he did it I simply thought he was a bit skittish, but such is the regularity of this show of aversion I am convinced he recognises her and harbours some instinctive mistrust. We have never witnessed him behaving like this to anyone else.

When I say Docker is my oldest friend, she really is. I met her, so to speak, before I can remember. Her mother is one of my mother's best friends so we go back a long way. And though our lives have taken very different paths, it is wonderfully reassuring when they do cross to have so very much shared history. At the moment, as we await her arrival, it crosses my mind that she may just be on a mission, encouraged by my mother, to see how we are settling in.

She has no children of her own, which I always think is a great pity as she is so good with mine. Unlike me, she will spend endless hours playing cards and board games with them; they are quite rightly excited about her visit. Joe sits in the garden so he can be the first to greet her, while Elfie is making biscuits for tea. Dan is up the tree in the drive and is planning an ambush.

For my part I'm relishing the prospect of a little adult conversation.

'Oh Docker, it's so good to see you. I'm so glad you're here. Tell me how are things in Devon? How's Aunty B?' I say as we make our way back from a walk along the beach.

'Everything's fine, but it's you I want to hear about. Mona's a bit concerned whether you're managing alright on your own.'

'I thought as much,' I say. 'And I'll be honest with you: I love the cottage and the village is great, but there are times . . .' I hesitate, 'but I would rather it didn't get back to Mum. Please don't tell her, she'll only worry . . .'

Docker smiles at me and I know it will go no further.

I take a breath, trying to marshal my thoughts. 'Today at lunch, you told me – not for the first time – what a wonderful life I lead, and to an extent you're right. I really do know how much I have going for me . . .'

'But?' says Docker.

'But . . . but . . . how do you describe a sense of loss? What I think you don't know is how desperately I miss Ben. I wished so much when he left that I could find it in my heart to hate him . . . to find faults and details of our life that would make me feel I was well rid of him. But I can't. Try as I may I never can. Even the way in which he conducted his affair, hurtful as it was, I could empathise with it. There was nothing clandestine or deceitful. It was reckless, unkind and destructive, yes. But there was a total honesty about it and for that I suppose I respect him . . .'

Docker says nothing, but her expression encourages me to go on.

'We were so intensely private in our years together, but I was blissfully happy sharing and knowing he was always around. Nowadays my diary makes pitiful reading, it's crammed full with details of the children's lives: triumphs, first words, teeth lost, achievements at school, parents' evenings and all with no one to share them with. I crab-fish, walk, bike, ride, picnic with the donkey, all of that, deliberately to make up for all the things I fear the children have missed out on. They are marvellous, so high-spirited. But there are times when I feel like Jekyll and Hyde. To the outside world I know I seem an exuberant outgoing sort of a person. But in the silence of home when I'm alone I often feel so inadequate and lose myself in dark thoughts . . .' I trail off, wondering if I've said too much; perhaps been a bit over-the-top.

'Oh Nicky,' says Docker, and I know she understands.

'So there we are, I've said it, sorry about that. Just please don't tell Mum.' And somehow, just for spilling it all out, I do feel better. 'Come on, let's get back for tea.'

*

Sharing a dormitory at school can make or break a friendship. In Sprat's case it was the former, and since those far off days we've been closer than siblings.

I don't think I'm a prude, but I am private. Years of boarding school went a long way to curing any natural coyness that may have been prevalent in my adolescent self. However, I like to think I afford my children a degree of privacy that was denied me. But Sprat is completely unselfconscious about, or should that be unaware of, her naked self. To the extent that she parades her Rubenesque nude body about the cottage while making us mugs of tea or collecting eggs for breakfast from the bottom of the garden. She is sublimely oblivious of the effect this has on my children, particularly the boys – their embarrassment is such they prefer to hide in cupboards rather than pass her in the corridor. They simply don't know where to look. However, Dan has a friend who is the complete opposite. He absolutely loves it and constantly asks when she is next coming to stay.

For myself, I have taken to locking the bathroom door of late; not something I would normally do. I am sick of the children barging in while I try to relax in the bath. It may not necessarily be to use the loo, but simply to tell me a snippet of school gossip or dob on a sibling or merely to sit on the floor for a chat. Whatever their motives, I find it increasingly intrusive, so now when I go for a bath I announce that I want a bit of peace and quiet and resolutely lock the door. This has resulted in the April child now calling a bath a 'peacelly quiet'.

And talking of baths, Sprat can never do anything by half. It's quite simply not in her nature.

'Be a love,' I say, 'and get the children in the bath. I must go and check on Doris.'

I return to hear squeals of delight from the bathroom and when I pop my head around the door, not only has she filled the bath with bubbles but is feeding the children great bunches of grapes. They are loving it.

She is here when we have our Halloween party. Joe can't sleep the night before, he is so excited at the thought of it. With the help of the children, Sprat completely transforms the dining room into a witches' cave, encouraging them to paint bats and spiders and all manner of ghoulish things all over the walls, while she hangs skeletons from the wooden beams. She even makes Joe a green bath and fills it full of plastic snakes and toads. I sometimes wonder how important these things are, and whether or not the children will remember them when they grow up. Sprat says I make magic for my kids. If that is so, she certainly eggs me on.

But I am beginning to see the advantages of being captain of my own ship. I can bang in nails where I wish and there's only me to mind if the shelf I put up is not straight.

Chapter 19

Gentle Joys

The dividing wall between the kitchen and the dining room has come down. At the same time I had a back door put in. This is a mixed blessing. On fine days it is left open and there is a continual procession of fowl, be it ducks or bantams strutting in in the hope of a morsel of food or some company. And it isn't exclusively poultry that avails itself of this facility; there have been occasions when the intruder was somewhat larger . . .

Recently I have been the recipient of two pieces of Portmeirion china. While not the sort of thing I would have bought for myself, I now quite like them. The larger bowl, decorated with passion flowers and ivy, sits resplendent on the Welsh dresser and is brimful of apples from the garden. I am mindful that pride is a deadly sin but I still think the greens against the pitched pine looks rather fine.

The kitchen door is wide open and the sun shines.

I am next door scrubbing the bath when I hear an unfamiliar noise. I listen for a moment before deciding to investigate and there in the kitchen is Rose, the donkey. It is apparent from the piece of chain hanging from her head collar that she has broken her tether. She is so engrossed in eating the apples from my new bowl that she is completely unaware of me. That is, until I wave my arms and shout at her. I should have thought first.

Off goes the donkey on her dainty little feet, trotting round the kitchen table and snatching at another apple on her way past the bowl.

I aim a slap on her rump, she bucks and the bowl crashes to the floor.

The next afternoon I make a huge batch of hummus; it's one of my specialities and even if I say so myself, it's delicious. Knowing Maggie loves it, I think I will take her some. I lift my other, smaller, Portmerion bowl down from the dresser and gaze admiringly at it. I deliberate as to whether or not to use it. Hesitatingly, I fill it up to the very brim, sprinkle it with paprika and drizzle olive oil over it. I call my daughter.

'Elfie darling,' I say, 'be a love and take this to Maggie, she's a bit down and it might cheer her up.'

At that moment Dan comes into the kitchen and volunteers to take it himself.

'It's okay,' I say. 'Elfie's taking it.'

'But I want to,' whines Dan.

'Why don't you both go?' I suggest.

The Elf picks up the bowl and the two of them set off down the path while I get on with things domestic. The next thing I know, Dan is tearing into the kitchen with his sister in pursuit screaming at him, and she's in tears.

'Whatever's the matter?' I ask.

'It's his fault,' she sobs.

'What are you talking about? Calm down.'

Apparently when they reached the gate, Dan tugged at the bowl, anxious to be the one to carry it. Elfie was resolute. Dan tried again and this time managed to prise the bowl from his sister's grip. She in turn pulled it back and between them they managed to drop the entire thing on the pavement. There seemed to be far more hummus on the pavement than was ever in the bowl. And it looked completely disgusting. And so it was that my second bowl was shattered.

Still, I always knew I wanted the dynamics of a family; not one solitary child but several. However much I bemoan my lot and the rigours of child-rearing, how glad I am that they are in the plural now that I am a single parent. There are enough of us to still feel like a proper family. And I relish the fact the children have each other to talk to, share experiences and to look out for each other.

If I could have only one tree in my garden, without a doubt it would be a Bramley apple tree. We inherited one with our cottage. It stands right outside the kitchen window and is a constant joy whatever the season. In the spring it is garlanded in the palest pink blossom giving the garden an altogether festive air. It is host to every garden bird I can identify. And year upon year it groans with enough apples to keep us and neighbours through until the following spring. The children pick up the windfalls and sell them at the gate, thus earning pocket money. It is even big enough for a swing yet the branches are low and generous for the children to practise their climbing skills.

For sheer visual pleasure I think perhaps a quince tree would come a close second. The unopened buds resemble tiny striped pink humbugs before they open into the most delicate of blossom. In the autumn it is hung with huge yellow quinces that are often mistaken for pears. And then there is the smell: like ripe pineapples and the garnet-coloured jelly. Yes, they are the most generous of trees.

As I wash up I muse on the delights of the garden. But my omniscient eye misses little.

'Darling, what are you doing?' I mouth through the kitchen window.

The April child is standing on an upturned box by the water butt. He's poking the surface but I can't quite see why.

I open the window and shout.

He doesn't answer, just goes on stirring with a stick.

I rush out into the garden for a better look and there bobbing about are the latest batch of guinea pig babies.

'I just wanted to see if they could swim,' he says.

Thank goodness I got there in time.

Elfie is going on an adventure holiday with the school – it sounds terrific. (I'd like an adventure holiday too!) There is great excitement and a pile of clothes to be labelled. Elfie seems more interested in whether or not they will be allowed pillow fights, and what might she take for midnight feasts, than any of the planned activities. I try to explain these things don't need permission; the very fact that they are illicit adds to the frisson of excitement.

There are times when I am appalled by my children. They display no spirit whatsoever. I cannot believe that I not only had to explain what a stink bomb is, but then had to go and actually buy them some.

The Elf let one off on the school bus, only because I said what a laugh we used to have with them. Predictably, she was hauled up in front of the headmaster. Now, it's good that she doesn't lie, I'm pleased about that. But couldn't she massage her imagination just a little, if only to protect me from the ire of her teachers.

She longs to be naughty, but it just doesn't come naturally to her. To Dan, yes. Joe, as yet undeveloped!

I'm sitting at the table sewing on name tags when Dan appears at the kitchen door with an open book.

'Did you know the longest bogey in the world was 68 cm?' he says with delight.

'No, I didn't and nor do I want to. You're so disgusting. Why can't you read a nature book instead of that one?' I ask.

'Nature doesn't interest me, and anyway you gave me this. It's called *Disgusting Facts*. Do you want to hear this one?'

'No, push off.'

Elfie shall have all she needs for pillow fights and midnight feasts. I remember how I loved sleeping away from home: lights out and torches and talking until midnight.

Meanwhile, I'm wondering whether sending Dan to his room is punishment or not. He doesn't seem to mind in the least. He always has some project on the go. At the moment it's painting lead figures and they are quite exquisite; I'm intrigued at how intricate his brushwork becomes. He showed me some tiny little *Star Wars* characters he's painting as a present for Joe . . . I rather hope as a peace offering after their latest run-in.

And it has suddenly dawned on me why nothing will grow in the flower border outside his bedroom window . . . Why do little boys delight in peeing anywhere that takes their fancy? As I write this, I can see my boys with two of their friends standing on the well wall and seeing who can pee the furthest. Come to think of it, male dogs are the same: constantly lifting their legs and marking their territory.

*

And now the children are going back to school. Joe for the first time. There is a tiny pang of nostalgia as I watch him line up for the bell, but then he is gone and with him, to my surprise, goes the pang. For ten years I have had a child around constantly, albeit with some help from time to time. The thought of endless childless uninterrupted hours stretching before me is bliss. Mum says I must be careful and leave something for myself when the children have grown up. I'm not sure I understand what she means. But whatever, it seems a long way off.

In the meantime there is a wonderful rightness knowing they will all be home for tea and homework and chaos, but home. They are my sole reason for living at the moment. The sun shines on. Joe will just be getting on the return bus and I am all a tizz of anticipation at the thought of that little beaming face returning. I shall skip to the bus stop feeling euphoric that I have sat at my typewriter and resisted all manner of delightful domestic chores.

It's half past six. The children are all fed and I have washed up. Joe plays, Dan is at his homework. He is learning to sew – his homework is a very pretty bit of needlework. At first I thought he was making me a mat, but no, when it is finished it is to be folded in two, sewn up the sides and become a pencil case. Dan, more than the others, has come on in leaps and bounds. He is so responsible nowadays. If anything, he takes it all too seriously.

Meanwhile Elfie practises the piano without being asked. I am making lemon curd, the children's favourite thing for breakfast. God is in his heaven and all of that. I am overcome by how fortunate I am.

'Joe darling,' I ask, 'what do you think of school dinners, do you like them?'

'I love them; today I had seconds of custard.'

'But I thought you didn't even like custard,' I say somewhat indignantly.

'But this was hot custard,' he replies.

As I try to recall my aptitude for custard making, he adds, 'And there were no lumps.'

Joe will be five tomorrow. I'm sure I bore everyone with what a delight he is. But arriving as he did, just as his father upped sticks and left me broken-hearted, I'm not sure I could have coped with another Dan. I'll rephrase that: I *know* I couldn't have coped with another Dan, much as I love him.

I go into Joe's bedroom to kiss him goodnight, his little freckled face beaming up at me as I bend down to him. Tucked into one side of him is his favourite soft toy, an Ewok – a grotty little character from *Star Wars* with huge eyes. For a moment I cannot distinguish between the two.

'Darling,' I say, 'do you realise this is the last time I shall kiss you as a four-year-old? Tomorrow you'll be a whole year older.'

I admit I may be erring a tad on the side of sentimentality, but there are times when I simply can't help myself. I get my come-uppance, however, when he bursts into uncontrollable tears.

'Whatever's the matter, darling?' I ask. 'It's your birthday tomorrow and we're having a party. Why the tears?'

'I don't want to grow up,' he snivels. 'I want to stay this age forever.'

'Why ever not?' I say as I wrap my arms around his little sobbing form.

'Because when I grow up I won't love you anymore.'

'What are you talking about?'

'When I'm grown up, I'll get like Ben. I'll start to hate you like he does. And I want to love you forever.'

What goes on in young minds? How much do they over-hear? Despite closed doors and lowered tones, how much do these innocents take in? What damage are we selfish, indul-gent, spoilt adults doing to the next generation? Elfie, too, is obviously upset by the divorce; she once asked me very simply if you could base your own happiness on making four others so desperately unhappy. I am in no doubt that she has lost her childhood.

Joe is so sweet. I'm sure no one could have a more loving child. He really has been a gift. Yes, I spank his bottom; I've even chased him with the whip, although I have no intention of using it. But without a doubt he is pure joy. Everyone loves him; if I could make a mould and cast lots of him I would have no more money worries.

He is bringing home some friends for his birthday tea. I have Thomas the Tank Engine tablecloths for the boys and Flower Fairies for the girls. Ben would have a fit, but for once I'm glad he's not here, so I can indulge the children as much as I jolly well want. Yippee! The cake is a masterpiece, a great blob of disgusting green cake balanced precariously on a shop-bought Swiss roll onto which I have meticulously stuck pieces of Cadbury's Flake to resemble bark. And it looks every bit as ghastly as it sounds. It's supposed to be an Acorn Green house and I shall surround the base with all the tiny Acorn Green characters. The candles are to be held in place by fresh primroses. Once again I remember Sprat saying I make magic for my children and how important that is.

I'm not sure if this is magic, but it's such a pleasure to do as I imagine all those little enchanted faces. Oh sad day, when no one wants your wizardry.

Joe's birthday tea is a delight. He is enraptured by his cake. At the last minute I had a brainwave. I gathered loads of tiny blue speedwell, which I found growing through some moss beneath the crab apple tree, and tucked this around the base of the chocolate 'tree' to look as if it was actually growing. Then I stuck as many figures as I could find amongst the greenery. It does look enchanting, but then to my horror tiny beetles and bugs started climbing about and getting trapped in the butter icing. Finally it is ready and the children are fascinated. It was well worth the effort. Joe gazes at it in wonder, quite speechless, and then his little voice pipes up, very slowly and hardly audible.

'Oh thank you Nick, thank you,' he whispers.

Chapter 20

The Picnic

We are picnicking in the forest. It has become a family ritual. On the last day of every holiday and every half term, Maggie and I take the children to the river. They paddle, make dams, fall in, get soaked and muddy, put nature in jars and generally do the stuff of childhood.

Maggie has brought along Sophie and James, and we also have Zoë, a family friend. Dan, for once, is elsewhere, staying with a mate.

There is more than one way to the river. Depending on the weather and our mood, either we drive a mile along the St Helena road, park and walk a further mile down a steep hill, or we trek by the church, along a lane, past a heap of sticks known as Eeyore's Place and eventually come to the river. It's by far the longer route, but does lend a feeling of adventure to the expedition.

Lately Rose the donkey has joined us on these trips. Our favourite journey is by Rose and cart, with all the children piled on top. But today is too muddy for the cart, so it's Rose and panniers, two large basketsful of rugs, wellies, microscopes, bottles of wine and Maggie's ubiquitous hard-boiled eggs, without which no picnic would be complete. We all groan when she unpacks them.

We have done with the picnic; the children have reached a satisfactory state of muddiness. I untie Rose from her bramble bush and position the panniers across her honest little back. Elfie and Zoë are at her head; she can be willful. I tighten her girth, secure the panniers, then lead her up to the pile of things Maggie has begun to pack. The little ones are playing Pooh-sticks.

'Where's Joe?' I ask. 'Joe?' He's nowhere to be seen.

'Perhaps he's gone for a pee,' suggests James.

'Quick, Sophie, look under the bridge,' I say. *Maybe he's fallen over in the water . . .*

'He isn't there,' says Sophie.

'Are you sure? . . . Joe!' I shout at the top of my voice.

We all listen to the silence.

'Elfie, you go that way,' I say, pointing up the hill. 'Zoe, you go back the way we came. He can't be far.'

I stand clutching the donkey's lead-rein, unclear as to what to do first.

'Joe,' I yell again. 'Maggie, here, you hold the donkey. Take the panniers off in case they slip. You'd better stay here. I'll try that way.'

Rose is very much a one-person donkey and starts fretting the moment I leave. Maggie gets asthma from animal hair.

I run about two hundred yards then return to question the others. *Compose yourself,* I think. He can't have disappeared that quickly, he was with us only minutes ago.

Elfina runs back out of breath. 'I've been all the way to the top of the hill and there's no sign of him.'

Composure to the wind, I rush off in Zoë's direction, leaving Maggie with a now boisterous donkey.

I meet Zoë coming back. 'I've been as far as Eeyore's Place,' she says, 'he's nowhere.'

'Joe!' I scream. 'Zoë, you go back and help Maggie with the little ones.'

I run along the track to the edge of the forest and double back on an open ride, then take another way down to the river. I question two families of walkers. No one has seen him. Back at the bridge I decide the first thing to do is get the donkey home and organise help. The situation is ludicrous: we are miles from anywhere with three children under six and one of them is lost.

'Maggie, you stay here in case he turns up.'

Elfie appears, red-faced and anxious. 'He's absolutely nowhere,' she says.

I grab the rope, pick up a large stick and make off with Rose. She's in no mood to trot. I whack her across the quarters just as one of the families I've questioned appears around a bend. They stare aghast. There isn't time to explain.

I look about me and see so many paths, so many potential wrong turns. *Where is he? What do I do? I'll phone the local policeman, that's what. Yes, he'll know how to organise a search party.* 'Come on Rose, come on.'

I'm exhausted, unfit, my stomach hurts and my face burns. I look at my watch. It's 4.15. There are three more hours of daylight.

I couldn't bear life without Joe. He's been such a joy. What's the date? March 31st. If they find him tomorrow it'll be April 1st. That's it . . . it's all a joke. It's not true, he's not even seven. How can he have disappeared so quickly? Why doesn't he answer?

We used to joke about him coming from the forest. We teased him, he was so gullible. Told him that's where we found him; not under the proverbial gooseberry bush like other children. One day we were going to return him to the forest where he belonged.

How could we have joked about it? He'll be terrified. Oh God, where is he? Perhaps his little body is lying in the undergrowth at this minute.

I pass more walkers. 'Have you seen a child?' I ask. 'He's lost. If you see him, please take him to the village . . . the museum . . . the shop . . . they all know him.'

I run on. The donkey senses my panic and begins to buck. I whack her on her rump again. As we pass the church my mind is racing, wondering what to do first.

I pass countless holidaymakers, some poised to take pictures of the donkey. I resist telling them what to do with their cameras.

Finally we reach home and there, standing by the gate, is a small muddy boy.

He says 'Hello Nick,' in the manner of someone who's been hanging around gates all his life.

I yell at him. 'What the hell are you doing there? Get in the car while I put Rose in the stable.'

He bursts into tears.

'Get in the car and shut up!'

The family who earlier caught me beating the donkey now witnesses me screaming at my child. They hurry past.

I bundle the donkey into the stable, then dash into the house to collect the keys.

'Where on earth have you been?' I shout as I slam the door shut. 'How the hell did you get home?'

'I got a lift, someone picked me up,' he says, trembling on the back seat.

'You what?' I mouth, turning around to look at him.

'A nice old lady stopped her car when I was on the road and asked if I was lost. I said, yes I am and I live at Bramley Cottage, the one with the wagon in the garden. So I got in and she brought me here,' he sobs.

'I don't believe it. You just got in a car with a stranger. How many times have you been told never to do that?' I shout.

He whispers, 'Oh yes, now I remember.'

I drive towards St Helena with frantic thoughts still coursing through my mind. We meet the Elf and Zoë halfway along the road. They look exhausted.

I stop the car. 'Jump in, he's here, he's safe.'

The girls get in and now Elfie starts yelling at her cowering sibling. She tells me they met two people on bikes who'd seen a child wandering along the road swinging his bag. They thought he looked a bit young to be on his own, but as he wasn't distressed they presumed he knew where he was going.

I park the car in the usual place and send the girls ahead to tell Maggie. 'Carry what you can to help her,' I call after them. 'I'll get the rest.'

Joe holds my hand as we follow. 'Why are you all so angry?' he sobs. 'I thought you'd be pleased to see me.'

'What made you run off like that, darling?'

'I wanted to be the first one home. I didn't know I'd come the wrong way till I saw the road.'

'So why on earth didn't you turn back?' I ask.

'I thought you'd all be home and I'd miss you.'

'But you knew we had the donkey and we'd gone the other way.'

'Oh yes,' he pondered for a moment, 'but I forgot.'

As we talk my eyes are drawn into the darkness, the infinity between the trees. I become aware of tracks previously un-noticed. I cling to the little hand.

'I thought you'd forget about me, that you wanted me to live in the forest,' he gulps through his tears.

I stop and cuddle him.

We reach the others and all flop down on the riverbank exhausted. The late afternoon sun mingled with the heady scent of pinewood seeps into us, reviving our strength. There is much talk of wandering off, of not getting into cars with strangers, but the little ones don't seem to listen.

'Where's Rose?' asks James. 'You said I could ride her home. Can it be my turn next?'

A hot bath and lots of cuddles later, I wish Joe goodnight. 'Darling, don't ever, ever run off again.'

'Ssh . . . don't talk about it . . . I don't want to remember,' he whispers. 'I didn't really come from the forest, did I?'

Chapter 21

Dull Women

I have just waved goodbye to a friend of a friend. I am euphoric at her departure. She was constantly welling up and bursting into tears. 'I so miss the male energy,' was her plaintive cry. It dawned on me, as she was describing yet another of her disastrous affairs, that women who have a great deal of relationships seem the most unhappy and unfulfilled of all.

During her stay the children did, against their better nature, keep chaos to a tolerable level. And very good-naturedly, I might add. But no sooner has she gone than we all lapse back to our everyday mode with a sigh of relief. Mayhem takes over once more, but I have kept my domain in order, washing up was done as required, floors swept, plants watered, things put away. By its very nature though, such a way of going on seems to prevent any other kind of interesting activity. I begin at last to grasp the correlation between immaculate houses and empty heads. It's not that I shouldn't like to live in a tidy house without dead plants. I don't enjoy endlessly stubbing my toes on Lego. But to keep on top of all the daily chores and then have the time and energy to explore the endless avenues that take our fancy is simply not possible.

I have nothing against housework and things domestic per se. I simply don't do it. Or at least I don't do it well. While I am washing the kitchen floor, I notice the cupboard doors are very grubby. As I am already on my hands and knees, I think I'll have a go at them. I squirt on some polish, which removes some but by no means all of the grime. I need a knife to chip off a variety of caked-on food. It takes me a good ten minutes to make it shine and very pretty it looks too. But not the drawer above, the bit below or indeed the doors on either side, not to mention the muddle behind the door. That's another matter altogether. Now, I think, I have an hour before Joe returns from school. And it occurs to me that if I clean some of the doors, not all, before he returns, I will not be fun and inspiring. I will be crotchety and dull. And six gleaming cupboard doors will only serve to show up all the un-gleaming ones. Also during my proximity to the floor I will notice holes in the linoleum and fantasise about changing it.

Or I'll notice a dirty mug in the bathroom. One little voice in my head says, 'Take it with you to the kitchen', while the other says, 'Oh bugger it, I'm not going that way, I can't be bothered.' The latter usually wins. I find it a constant effort to be tidy but I have to giggle at the second voice. Sometimes it seems to take over despite myself. Could this be the rebel who has constantly got me into scrapes? If so, I stand blameless; the matter is out of my court. Sometimes the effort to discipline my internal mutineer is simply too great. I think it must be my spirit; and all this vacillation over a measly cup of abandoned coffee!

Housework is all consuming . . . it feeds on itself. It sucks me in, and far from making me proud of my endeavours, it only serves to remind me of all the other bits left undone. A walk, on the other hand, will always feed my soul, lighten my spirit and negate this dreadful desire to control.

I have worked tirelessly on my attitude towards tidiness. I constantly quell any urge that may arise. It's not that easy. I'm not lazy, far from it; I just don't like wasting time on such mindless activities. I still don't know if you dust before or after vacuuming. I don't actually care. When Quentin Crisp, in *The Naked Civil Servant*, said that dust didn't get any thicker after four years, it was music to my ears; and by the way, he's right.

I buy a can of cobweb spray from a party shop. It should be just the ticket for decorating the dining room for Halloween. It is only when I am balancing precariously on top of the Welsh dresser; aiming the can into a corner of the beams, that I notice, to my delight, there are already webs far superior to anything the spray might produce. So I abandon that idea and instead spray the existing cobwebs with luminous paint and they glow in the dark. They are really effective, so much so that I now glitter-dust them at Christmas, and they've become quite a feature!

One wet day in the school holidays, Dan asks if he might use the dining-room table to build a Lego village. Obviously, I agree. Soon Joe asks if he can add his castle and knights. By the end of the day, the table – all ten feet of it – looks so splendid, with *Star Wars* fighting dinosaurs, versus My Little Ponies and so on . . . I quite simply don't have the heart to tidy it up, nor shall I acquire the heart for some months. We eat off our knees.

*

How I laughed when a friend gave me a mug, actually a very pretty blue and cream one, emblazoned with ONLY DULL WOMEN HAVE TIDY HOUSES. I was enchanted. What a wag, I mused, someone at last who sees beyond a bit of mess. I felt vindicated for what others perceived as chaos. I really warmed to my new best friend. At least she knew I had better things to do with my time.

Avoid things vexatious to the spirit, that's what I say. There follows a microcosm of my credo.

Picture a perfect June morning: I return from the school bus with armfuls of elderflower blossoms, intent on making cordial. With my own special alchemy this day will be captured in bottles to sustain us through the long winter months. The kitchen door is open; I carry a heavy bowl in the direction of the pantry at the precise moment the cat chooses to run in with a tiny rabbit in its mouth. I shout at him as he dashes past, then I trip, and two gallons of my sugary elixir is splashed liberally and literally everywhere, including over Puss. He immediately drops his prey and dashes off, shaking mess everywhere. The baby bunny charges, bewildered, behind a cupboard. Now even I am forced to apply a little domesticity to this pandemonium. But not before I recover the sugared bunny and find a cosy box for it (to die in, I think cynically). When at last I locate the mop and bucket, there is, to my delight, a small songbird nesting in it; and she's sitting! I can't possibly move her. Instead I find my bird book to try and identify exactly what she might be.

All this time the mess in the kitchen is becoming stickier by the minute, making clearing up ever more arduous. And before I know it the children are home from school and all my precious time has gone.

Really, what I should have done was lay down in a field

blotting up every last drop of such a day – instead of trying to bottle it.

One of my favourite friends is a musician; a highly intelligent one at that. And while I am not overly familiar with musicians as a group, I do have a healthy respect for their accomplishments. At a push, any of us could paint a picture of sorts, write an essay after a fashion, but unless one is a born genius I defy anyone to play a piece of music, on let us say, a piano, without a copious amount of practising.

It was she who gave me the most wonderful piece of advice. Being an earth mother to five robust embryonic trenchermen, baking their daily bread was a necessity. There are those who knead the dough until it 'feels right'. There are others who knead their dough for a set amount of time regardless of feeling anything. But for Julia a Concerto, either Mozart, Chopin, Schumann or Grieg, is the perfect length for her to knead her daily loaf into the exact consistency. But the benefits are more. She can vent her frustrations into the dough while her spirits soar to the strains of Mozart wafting through the house. And then she added, 'But I wouldn't bother with Brahms: he might be a weeny bit heftier and run on too long.' I love it. It's so lyrical.

Chapter 22

Apples

Now all the children are at school, it is imperative that I get a job. As I struggle to find employment that will pay anything more than the minimum wage, I am reminded once more that my cursory attitude towards education has resulted in an own goal.

I want to be there for my children. Whether or not they want me there is another matter, but it's imperative to me to be waiting for them at the end of their school day.

So, in the absence of anything more edifying, I have decided to start apple picking. I heard about it at the school gates. Not only are the orchards local but it appears this type of land work is traditionally done by women. As such the day finishes at three o'clock and so it sounds ideal for me.

I arrive at the farm at nine sharp, and despite recognising the odd mum from school, I don't actually know anyone. Conversely, they all seem to know everyone and are all chattering away. I feel unusually anxious as I make my way across the forecourt clutching a Thermos flask and my packed lunch. I am mindful of Joe and his first day of school.

Trevor the farm manager is quite obviously shy and blushes

readily. It is apparent he is not at his ease when faced with a bevy of sharp-tongued women.

He is also a man of few words. 'Morning,' he says. 'We're going to make a start on the coxes in the Four Acres, but don't start picking.' His manner is gruff. 'Wait till I get down there. I've a few things to explain.'

The tractors' engines are already running and the air is thick with the heady smell of diesel as we pile onto the back of the trailers. Once we are all settled on our upturned buckets amongst wooden crates, we are trundled off along bumpy tracks towards the orchards.

Initially I am struck by the beauty of the trees; boughs groaning with fruit, some almost touching the ground. I notice several of the trees have uprooted and fallen over, they are so top-heavy with apples.

Trevor arrives with a bundle of templates under one arm and a pile of photos under the other. Size matters, as does colour. We are each given a template as he explains that he only wants us to pick apples that fit precisely through the hole. No bigger and no smaller.

'And no greener than this,' he says, holding up a photo in his left hand. 'No redder,' says our man of words, waving the other picture.

A cold, dull start turns into a fine late summer day. A strong September sun beats down on us and soon we are as rosy-cheeked as the apples.

I had no idea that something as mundane as picking apples could be so thought-provoking. Constantly referring to our gauges slows us down, and like Goldilocks, we deliberate over each fruit until it becomes second nature.

When I query the reasoning behind such precision, the answer is simple.

'The housewife doesn't like too big an apple, and she won't buy them if they look over- or under-ripe,' says Trevor.

It appears the ubiquitous housewife is to blame for much that is wrong in farming nowadays.

Having worked our way through the orchards, picking only the very best, we then return to the beginning and are instructed to strip the trees completely. But this time, instead of being gently tipped into huge wooden crates, the offending fruit, the ones that are deemed unsuitable for consumption, are thrown unceremoniously on the ground. If I didn't need the money, all minimum wage of it, I should have protested and walked out at what follows.

A bulldozer drives up and down between the rows of trees pushing all the unwanted apples into huge heaps. It then drives backwards and forwards, crushing the discarded fruit to a pulp. I am appalled and say so. Surely they could be of use to someone I plead, but in vain. Apparently it is 'government intervention' – for what it's worth, or indeed what it means. And that is that.

Picking apples is boring, tiring and very hard work; it is interminable and my limbs ache. But oddly enough I love feeling physically exhausted; it enriches the rest of my day. Even a simple hot bath when I return home is transformed into a sensuous experience. I am really beginning to delight in the elements, the sheer joy of working out of doors with nature.

The oddest spin off of all, however, is that I am becoming less tolerant of the chaos in my life. I begin to question the muddle in which I operate. Surprisingly I no longer eschew housework as some middle-class phenomenon and actively engage in some serious blitzing of our little domain.

After three weeks of back-breaking work, the apple harvest

is over, at least for another year. Trevor approaches me on the last day and asks if I would be interested in coming back to prune the trees later in the autumn. While I know it will be even harder work, I am secretly thrilled to be singled out and reply a resounding 'Yes!'

What antisocial work pruning trees can be. More often than not the weather is freezing cold and windy, and I am aware that only the more diligent workers have returned. Nowadays people eulogise farm labour. While some of it may be worthy of such praise, I would suggest that in truth most of it is sheer drudge; land work is relentless. On wet days when we tire of pruning, we positively wish the hours to pass. That can't be right: to will our lives away.

It was during that winter, when I stayed on to prune, that I got to know Ethel better.

I had never seen anyone re-use the same tea bag for three days running. It fascinated me. I sat mesmerised by the plump, gnarled fingers as they fished around in the hot water, removed the bag and popped it into a little screw-top jar. As time went on, I realised this frugality was born of necessity.

Ethel worked on the land relentlessly, in all weathers, to pay the bills, unlike the rest of us to whom it was the icing on the cake, the leather jacket for the daughter, a video recorder, perhaps a microwave. No, to Ethel, work meant a roof over her head, the bills paid and, if there was anything left over, a new bike. A bike with gears, a bike that would help her along the four and a half dreary miles she had cycled on the same old bone shaker for her entire working life. She explained to me excitedly that with gears she could get up the modest hills without dismounting.

I was to learn some months later that Fred, her lay-about husband, owned a car. Why, I naively asked, if he was unemployed did he not run her to work? He charged her too much. On the rare occasions he took her to Lowestoft she would pay him, for both time and petrol. But it was not in Ethel's nature to complain; she accepted the blows fate dealt her, blows that to anyone else might have proved crippling. She took what life dealt her sublimely. It would never have occurred to her to grasp life firmly between her ample hands and steer her own path. Why should she, when she trusted it so implicitly?

On wet days she would arrive trussed up like a chicken; a spectacle of black bin liners and binder twine. Oblivious to sarcasm, the jokes, like the rain, washed over her. I think that is what I found so endearing. The other workers despised her, but she neither knew nor cared. Her pea-pod wine was the best it had ever been and that was enough.

The only thing I ever heard Ethel long for was a grandchild. She told me very quietly one day her first child was stillborn, and how sometimes the longing to hold a baby in her arms was painful. She allowed herself the one luxury of knitting exquisite little jackets; the soft pink wool in those large raw hands was somehow incongruous.

Ethel died as she had lived, with the minimum of fuss. She bicycled home, got Fred his tea as usual, wiped the dishes and sat down in her chair. She mentioned a pain in her chest, closed her eyes and was gone.

Apart from Fred, there were only three other people in church. Even the vicar forgot her name and hastily looked down at his notes. As I gazed at the coffin, I wondered why this tired, simple old lady so moved me. Why did I, who hates funerals, feel drawn to this one on a wet blustery December day?

We sang *Rock of Ages* and I thought of all the countless

Chapter 23

High Tides

As I've mentioned, I bought Bramley Cottage on an impulse; it felt right the moment I walked through the door, and it still does. The postman, however, asked me whatever had induced me to buy such a dump – had they given it away? He wouldn't live here himself even if it was gift-wrapped. I merely thought he was rather rude and overly familiar.

And then, when I spoke to the insurance company regarding cover for the cottage, the lady at the other end of the phone asked how close we were to the sea, approximately.

I looked out of the window as I spoke, and never having been good at estimating distance, said in all honesty about five hundred yards.

'Fine,' she said. 'I'll have your documents in the post tonight.'

I cannot remember how long I have been asleep when I am woken by the phone ringing. I glance at the clock by my bed and register 12.30. I make a mental check that all the children are here under my roof, so I pick the phone up with less apprehension than my initial reaction to a call at such an hour.

It is an automated voice. 'This is the Environmental Agency – this is a storm warning. There is a likelihood of strong tides and flooding along the east coast. Please be prepared.' And then the line goes dead.

I sit up in bed and listen. The wind is howling and through my open window I can hear the sound of waves crashing on the shingle then dragging back down to the sea.

I am completely unsure of what 'Please be prepared' can mean.

Outside on the road there is the unmistakable roar of a lorry followed by the screeching of brakes and slamming of doors. There is a definite hint of urgency in the voices coming up from the street. I jump out of bed and cross over to the window where, by the light of the moon, I can just make out the forms of two men.

I shout down to them to hang on a moment while I pull on some clothes.

When I reach my gate I recognise the two men as local fishermen, Stephen and Philip. They have begun to unload a pile of sandbags onto the drive.

'Good heavens! What does all this mean?' I ask.

'High tides! There's low pressure in the North Sea; we're in for some serious flooding,' shouts Stephen. 'It'll come into the gardens on your side of the street. I'd get started if I were you.'

'Start what?' I yell over the roar of the sea.

'Putting this lot around your doors. Not sure if it will be high enough to come into your house,' continues Philip, 'but I wouldn't put money on it. You never know till two hours after the tide turns.'

'What? The sea, come into the house? You can't be serious,' I say, while wondering quite what to do first.

'What do you think this lot are for love, if we're not serious?' says Philip, waving at the back of the lorry piled high with sandbags.

'But what does it all mean? What can I do?'

'Well, start stacking up this lot; they'll stop the water for a while.'

I bend down to pick one up and am horrified at how heavy they are.

'Here! Come on, we'll give you a hand,' says Stephen, tucking a sack under each arm and striding towards the kitchen door.

By now most of the menfolk in the street are up and about. There is a feeling of camaraderie as they rush about lugging sandbags off the lorry and piling them around any doorway that might be at risk from the incoming tide.

I go back into the house to check on the children, still unsure as to whether or not to wake them. I creep into Elfie's room where she sleeps on, gloriously unaware of the imminent drama unfolding around us. From her window I glance out towards the sea and with the light of the full moon can just make out the waves crashing over the sea wall.

A sense of panic rises in my chest. I swallow hard and remind myself to stay calm. Elfie must sense my presence and wakes up.

'Is that you, Nick?' she asks, rubbing her eyes. 'What's up?'

I sit down on her bed and take her hand. 'Darling, it's the sea.'

'What do you mean, the sea?'

'There's going to be flooding tonight. There are men out-side at the moment piling sandbags around the door.'

'I don't understand,' she says, getting out of bed and joining me at the window. Out across the bay the lighthouse flashes away as usual, but to our right, along the back of the beach, we can just make out the glinting froth of waves as they crash up and over onto the marshes. I wait until my eyes become more accustomed to the light and I stare at what looks like water seeping through a breach in the sea wall.

The phone rings again. I run down to my room and grab the phone. 'Hi, it's Maggie. Are you okay? Do you want Mick to come and help you?'

'Oh Maggie,' I say, trying not to let the panic show in my voice. 'I'm not sure what to think. We've done the sandbags but I don't know what to do next. I don't even know whether to wake the boys or not.'

'I would if I were you. Go and get them dressed and into something warm. Hang on, don't worry, we'll be there in a minute.'

I wake the boys and dress them hurriedly.

'Darling, the sea is very rough and there might be a flood,' I say to Joe.

'Like in Noah's Ark?' he asks excitedly.

'I hope not,' I say. 'Come on, I can hear Maggie at the door.'

We grab torches and leaning into a biting north-westerly wind, we all set off in the direction of the beach. I cling fast to the boys' hands while wondering if perhaps this isn't a little foolhardy. The children already have fertile enough imaginations without fuelling them further with the ferocious sea that greets us. It has already come in a good fifty yards further than the normal tide and, as we watch, a massive wave picks up a fishing boat and tosses it over the sea wall like a bit of flotsam.

'Wow, that's awesome,' says Dan. 'Is the tide going to come in any further?'

One of the fishermen who helped us with the sandbags overhears him. 'We don't know lad, but all the conditions are right for a massive surge tonight.'

'What do you mean?' I shout over the roar of the sea.

'If it's as bad as it looks it'll definitely be in your garden by the morning.'

'Does that mean us?' says the Elf.

'I think so, darling. Perhaps we'd better get back.'

'What about the animals?' she asks.

'Tell you what, we'll come back with you,' says Maggie. 'We'll give you a hand.'

'That would be great, but haven't you got enough to do of your own?'

'Well that's the point; we're on the other side of the road. We're okay.'

Anticipating the worst, the first thing I do is to position the car in readiness for a quick getaway. The Elf is rightly concerned about Bun and Puss. With Maggie's help, they are caught up and spend the night sitting patiently on the back seat awaiting a hasty departure.

I set the boys to taking anything of value (to them) upstairs, while Mick and I pile sofas, and anything else that may suffer from a soaking, on tables.

By the time Mick and Maggie have left us, the house looks like a saleroom with furniture and books stacked up all over the place.

We are too excited to sleep and instead the children all huddle up in my bed and drink mugs of tea.

But we must have fallen asleep for the next thing I know it's daylight. I jump out of bed and run down the corridor to Elfie's room. From the north-facing window I stare out towards the marshes. They are completely underwater. I lower my gaze to our garden and am unsure whether to be relieved or not. The tide has quite obviously stopped and turned just by the old apple tree, halfway up the garden. And there, as if for proof, is a line of flotsam, anything that could be swept along on the relentless tide. From the size of some of the pieces of wood, I deduce how powerful the tide must have been. Out in the drive I spy Puss and Bun staring patiently out of Noah's Ark with rather bemused looks on their faces.

The children sleep on. There will be no school today.

Chapter 24

Village Scenes

Some local amateur historian has just discovered that in medieval times, on the feast of St James, there was a street fair in the village. So it's been decided to resurrect the custom to raise some much needed funds for both the church and museum.

We have all been urged to think of original ideas. I ask the children if they would like to get involved and am amazed at their input. Not only do they rise to the challenge, but the ideas they come up with are brilliant.

Rather appropriately, Dan has been learning medieval history at school and suggests a court jester. He himself is at an age when he would prefer to dress up as a knight but can see no reason why his younger brother wouldn't make an excellent wit! Given their diminutive size it is decided that Joe and James, Maggie's youngest, should both be wits . . . half-wits.

'I think that's inspired, Dan, but you'll have to find some nice easy jokes – clean ones – that they can remember.'

We set to work making costumes. I knit Dan some chain mail out of dishcloth cotton and spray it silver. Then I rip up an old sheet to make a tabard and leave him to paint it with a St George cross. Maggie is the seamstress and makes the little ones bright yellow and red outfits. Ingeniously she has cut two T-shirts and two pairs of tights up the middle and re-sewn them in opposite colours – they look masterful. When I finish my knitting, I set about sewing bells onto the little jester outfits to complete the look.

Dan is coaching Joe and James with their jokes. They are to charge a penny a joke and are struggling to remember more than three each.

'Joe, what do you call a chicken in a shell suit?'

'An egg.'

'Well done. How do hens dance?'

They both shrug their shoulders.

'Chick to chick.'

'Last one: what do you call two robbers?'

'I don't know.'

'A pair of knickers,' says Dan.

'I don't get that,' whines Joe.

'I don't get any of them,' says James.

I'm not sure how Dan is planning to earn money, but he is so pleased with his armour he is running about the garden swiping the heads off all my hollyhocks with a sword he's just made.

He does eventually put a joke bloody finger in a matchbox and pretends it's a relic he's brought back from the Crusades, and is to charge any unsuspecting soul to have a look.

Elfie has decided to make bed bugs. To say I am fascinated is putting it mildly.

Firstly I cannot imagine how she even has heard of, let alone knows, what a bed bug is. I admit we have played host to the odd flea, usually courtesy of the cat. But bed bugs? I'm not sure I even know what they look like.

The table is covered with watermelon pips. They have been drying in the airing cupboard for days. She picks one up and tells me to have a good look at it. I do but am not sure what I'm supposed to say.

'Look carefully,' she continues. 'Can you not see that little bit of black at the tip?'

I look again. 'Yes, so what?'

'So,' she says, 'doesn't it look like a little eye to you? I'm going to stick bits of cotton on them like legs.'

'Don't be daft – why do you want to do that?' I ask.

'I'll find out the Latin name for them and sell them as medieval bed bugs.'

I am loath to quell such quirky enthusiasm, while secretly glowing with maternal pride.

With a diligence that can only be matched by her imagination, my daughter then proceeds to create hundreds of tiny pests. I help her to wrap each one carefully in a scrap of handmade paper. Then, when she has stamped each tiny packet with sealing wax, I scrawl *Leticularis Dunwichiensis* across the front in a spidery hand.

On the day of the sale she puts a bed bug in one of those little microscopes for viewing nature. They look utterly convincing. So much so they are a sell-out. Ingeniously she only allows people to buy one each, suggesting that two might breed and infest their house. Not only are people intrigued, but are completely taken in.

Caroline, who lives along the road, has turned her kitchen into a bakery. It has a stable door that opens directly onto the street so will be ideal. We are to stay up all night and bake rustic-looking bread.

Elfie and her friend Vanessa make batch after batch of little buns that they are to ice patriotically. I leave them to get on with it while I go and make bread.

When I return, the girls have already gone to bed but there in front of me is their baking. They have made dozens of little cakes and they are iced, though not with the cross of St George that I was expecting. Instead I stare in horror: there on the table is tray after tray of buns iced with big, black swastikas.

My contribution appears quite tame compared to the children's. I've found someone who can tell fortunes. Given that I not only own a gypsy wagon and a crystal ball, it's a pity not to have them as the star attraction. I'm not sure when fortune telling began; it doesn't exactly have a very medieval resonance to it. But hey! Does it matter? It will be great fun and I'm convinced it will prove a huge success.

Years ago my mother returned from Morocco laden down with a huge pair of panniers for me. When I first caught sight of her at the airport I was quite taken aback and wondered whatever had come over her. But that was then; I now think they are wonderfully useful. Admittedly it helps if you have a donkey to strap them to. Normally we use them for picnics or gathering firewood in the forest, but now I have the inspired idea of filling them with oranges to sell to the hordes of visitors. Rosie will look very decorative and I shall wander about selling my wares.

At least this might look more medieval, I think reassuringly to myself. That is until some pedant queries the oranges. Honestly, it is possible to take things a little too seriously.

On the day of the fair we all dress appropriately; there are village stocks, and goats and chickens mingle freely through the crowds. It all looks terrific.

I harness Doris to the wagon and drive her down to the field allocated for the hub of the proceedings. In one corner is Barney, Caroline's son, who along with some mates has volunteered to oversee the roasting of a sheep . . . Anxious that it should not be undercooked, they have stayed up all night keeping vigil. I notice they lie asleep by the fire surrounded by empty bottles.

I am banging in the stake to tether Doris to when Judy, a friend of the fortune teller, approaches me, all flushed and out of breath.

'Oh thank heavens! There you are! We have a problem, Nicky,' she says, gasping for air.

'Whatever's up? Here, sit down,' I say, patting the steps to the wagon.

'It's the fortune teller. I'm afraid she can't do it,' she says as she plonks herself down on the bottom step. 'Her mother's just died. Completely unexpected.'

'Well, she can't have been much of a fortune teller if she didn't see that one coming,' I laugh, amused with my quick wit.

She looks at me with her mouth open and says nothing.

Not satisfied with my complete lack of tact I go on, 'Sounds like divine retribution for dabbling in the occult, don't you think?'

It appears she is lost for words. She stands up and walks away.

As the wagon is already in the field, I decide to simply let people sit in it for a small fee. To most people wagons are still a novelty and I'm convinced this will prove a good money-spinner, despite the absence of a soothsayer.

I unharness Doris and lead her over by the hedge to tether her. I am already dressed in my fetching little hessian number complete with no shoes when my horse, all half ton of her, steps forward right onto my bare foot.

I hobble up the road with blood running freely and what I suspect are broken toes. I am still wondering if I can get to hospital and back before the fair gets underway when I reach the cottage. The children are already dressed up in their various costumes and are so excited that I don't have the heart to disappoint them with my problem. Instead I bandage my foot as tightly as I can and limp about selling my wares.

It is a memorable day, everyone contributing and doing their bit. It seems to bring the entire village together, both old and young in a very unique way. But it is on our little half-wits that the greatest praise is heaped. Not only did they raise money with their joke telling, they brought a smile to everyone's face.

Our village church has an annual nativity play that I now help to organise. It's about the only time in the year when all the local children get together and inevitably results in the usual bedlam of squealing angels and scratchy recorders. Why not, I think in a moment of inspiration, let Mary and Joseph arrive by donkey? After all, it has been done before.

With a healthy respect for Rose's single-mindedness, I think it wise to rehearse the previous week to prepare her for her all-important role. With an empty church and a bucket of carrots she was exemplary. But what, I wonder, might she be like when it is packed full of festive cheer. Not daring to trust her to an eight-year-old Joseph, I decide in the interests of safety it would be better to lead the little trio to Bethlehem myself.

It is dark and cold standing in the graveyard. Mary and Joseph shiver, their bare feet are blue with cold. We wait in silence for our moment. Then the huge wooden door swings open and the organ strikes up 'Little Donkey'. My heart is in my mouth as I lift Mary onto Rose's back. She doesn't flinch at all, instead peering into the unfamiliar glaring light. As the first words of the carol strike up, we enter slowly, cautiously, Joseph on one side and me holding firmly onto her bridle on the other.

Instead of her usual wilfulness, Rose seems to know exactly what is expected of her and calmly sets off on her journey towards the altar. There, eagerly awaiting the arrival of the happy couple, is a colourful assortment of angels, shepherds . . . with the odd token sheep.

Few of the children knew that Mary was to arrive thus so their faces are truly faces of wonder and delight. They watch enchanted as this humble timeless creature picks her way daintily down the aisle. How could I have mistrusted her? – she knew it all.

As the last lines of the song drift away, Mary and Joseph are carefully deposited among their retinue of helpers, and Rose and I strike a hasty retreat to the back of the church.

After the last carol has echoed out around the rafters, a mum corners me and says, 'What a delightful service, didn't the children do well.'

Then she adds, 'But it never occurred to me that Mary and Joseph would have had a chauffeur.'

Chapter 25

Flourishing

Despite being in the rudest of health, the bantams Sidney and Toots have failed to produce more than one clutch of chicks, and one of those isn't really worth writing home about. We christen her Maisy. Maisy is a sickly infant and had it been her fate to have hatched anywhere other than here, I doubt she would have survived. As it is, Sprat is staying the Easter weekend that Maisy first puts in an appearance. It is apparent right from the start she is not quite the full shilling. But rather than leave her to fate, Sprat tucks the tiny chick down her bra and we all go off to church. Whenever it lets out a tiny plaintive cheep, we all peer down Sprat's front as she feeds it from a little pipette.

The spectacle of the boys gazing with such intensity down her, not insubstantial, cleavage draws some very disapproving looks from the congregation. And I quite think it makes the vicar's day when Sprat asks him, on our way out of church, if he too would care to take a peep.

I have learnt from bitter experience that interfering with nature can often be counterproductive, not to mention heartbreaking. But Maisy proves the exception. Not only does she survive, but she grows up to be a bantam of such character that she inspires Joe to write his first school essay.

A SHORT BIOGRAPHY OF A CHICKEN
by J. H. aged seven

Born in Dunwich after 21 days of Toots sitting on her, she had two brothers, Wilfred and Erbet. Maisy grew up in a battle zone between her two brothers and her father Sidney, but never seemed to notice the constant fights; she just carried on having dust baths and leading her quiet life.

Maisy never quite got on with Sidney and always would tag along hoping for some food which Toots didn't want. Wilfred did the same and soon brother and sister were to fall in love.

This relationship went on for her life but her egg laying didn't. One day I was feeding the chickens when I looked in the garage and there was Maisy sitting there looking at an egg, not sitting on it, looking at it. After about two days she gave up, never to try again for the rest of her life. Instead she would sit under the kitchen table and chat to Wilfred about the day's events.

While Joe appears to be thriving at school, there are times when he manifests a vagueness which can charm or annoy in equal measure.

'Is that Joe's mum?' says the voice at the other end of the phone.

'Yes,' I reply, 'who's speaking?'

'It's Pam from Middlefield School.'

Before she can say any more I panic and interject, 'Is everything all right? Has there been an accident?'

'No, it's nothing like that. I just wanted to say that this morning Joe arrived at school in his stocking feet. He's forgotten his shoes.'

'I know,' I say. 'I took him to the bus stop.'

There is a silence at the other end of the phone. 'I'm sorry, I don't understand. You put him on the bus with no shoes?'

'Yes,' I reply while wondering what else I can say.

'So you don't mind?'

'It's not that I don't mind,' I say. 'He will keep playing in the mornings and I'm fed up telling him to get dressed. This morning when I said, "Come on get in the car", he couldn't find his shoes. Frankly, I think it's the only way he will learn.'

There is nothing but a stunned silence on the other end of the line.

I am in the kitchen preparing tea when Joe comes in with paper and pencil. Without saying a word to me, he starts to count the books. I notice there are already some numbers written on his scrap of paper.

'What are you doing, darling?'

'It's my homework.'

'What is?'

'Mrs Bateman said she wanted us to count how many books we have.'

'Do you mean like children's books?' I ask.

'No, she wants to know how many books we have in our house,' he says, then continues counting.

I suppose it's good for his arithmetic, I muse, as I roll out some pastry.

'Nick,' says Joe the next evening, 'you know I had to count books yesterday? Well Mrs Bateman didn't believe me.'

'What do you mean she didn't believe you? What did you say?'

'I told her we had two thousand and sixty. And she said I must have counted wrongly. So I have to do it all over again. I don't think that's fair. Then I remembered I'd forgotten the ones in your bedroom. Can I go and count those?' he asks.

But Joe uses the word 'bored' too regularly. I don't remember the others saying they were bored. I'm fascinated to see how this develops. He's become more outspoken since he started school. That dear little loving child is changing rapidly. Perhaps in many ways it's a good thing, but sad how quickly they grow up.

The Elf is growing up too, and has devised a cunning way of making money. Whenever I have people for supper she produces the hamster. She plonks him in the middle of the table and regardless of the reaction from some, she proceeds to ask if anyone wants to bet on how many peanuts it can get in its mouth at one time. We all know about a hamster's capacity to hold food in its cheeks but my unsuspecting guests are about to get a shock.

I have tried to dissuade my daughter from gambling; it's not an asset I would have desired in one so young, but she doesn't listen.

Instead she begins to place peanuts down the table, around glasses, wine bottles or whatever obstacle is in her path.

'Come on, Docker,' she says, 'how many nuts do you think Berry can pick up in one go?'

'I reckon about ten,' says Docker sportingly.

'Well if you're right I'll give you ten pence, but if not you've got to give me a penny for every nut he picks up, okay?' says my twelve-year-old daughter.

'That sounds easy money,' says Richard, 'you're on. I say fourteen.'

And so it goes, until all my guests who have not yet witnessed this phenomenon have placed their bets.

I roll a fag and lean back in my chair wondering where this gambling streak in my first-born has come from.

Elfie puts Berry down amongst the plates. We all watch intently as he scuttles towards his first peanut. He twitches his nose then shovels it in . . . then the next . . . then another . . .

Someone starts counting, 'Six . . . seven . . .' as we watch Berry dodge behind the wine bottles.

'Twelve . . . thirteen . . . oh surely that's it! Oh look at his poor little mouth.'

The Elf flashes me a knowing look, and winks.

'Well that's me out,' says Mick. 'Sixteen, good God, I wouldn't have thought it possible! He's up to twenty-four now.'

Tonight he has managed twenty-eight; not quite a record, but close. I feel a warm glow of maternal pride as I watch my first-born pocket her money, scoop up the hamster and bid us all a fond goodnight.

Dan, meanwhile, so wants to be the man of the house. There are times when he assumes responsibilities beyond his years. Daily he grows more thoughtful and recently has taken to helping Joe with his homework. His birthday is February 14th. I think it a wonderfully auspicious date and for years the theme of his tea hasn't wavered. This year he's invited some school friends to a party. I have hired the *Ghostbusters* video as the focus of the afternoon and there is much excitement. But he's begged me in no uncertain terms, 'Please Nick, please don't make me any heart-shaped biscuits or cake ever again. They are so soppy.'

Thinking the video may be a little scary for nine-year-olds, I ask the relevant parents' permission first. They all agreed it would be fine. But when I go into the sitting room to see how they are all enjoying it there is no one in evidence. Then, slowly, four terrified little faces appear from behind the sofa.

'Tell you what,' I say, 'why don't we just go and get on with tea?'

They leap at my suggestion.

Chapter 26

The Interest Table

While I am no tree hugger and certainly not a vegetarian, I do love the natural world. Mosquitoes annoy me and I react badly to wasp stings but in general, I would sooner study an insect than kill it. I am delighted to note I have engendered some of this appreciation in my children.

Most of the teachers from my school days are completely unmemorable. They seemed rather a sad bunch of uninspiring, disillusioned spinsters. With hindsight I realise teaching was probably their only option in life.

The exception was Miss Cobbley or 'Cobbles' as she was known affectionately. Her domain was the science laboratory, but she also taught biology and botany. Her enthusiasm for her subjects was contagious and it was impossible not to be swept up in her wake. She was enchanting, but perhaps this is on reflection. At the time, if my memory serves me right, we teased her mercilessly. But she remained gloriously unaware, such was her passion for the natural world; be it dissecting the sexual organs of a frog or trailing us miles across the Sussex Downs to look at bee orchids.

🖉 We had seen the bee orchids, charming elusive little things that they were. Too shy to bloom where they might be seen, we had to trek miles over the Sussex Downs, up hills and down dales. And just where Miss Cobbley said they would be, they were and had been for centuries. Not that any of us were really terribly interested. We had joined the Botanic Society purely for the jaunts it promised. I expect we would have joined the Euthanasia Society had it offered a bus trip with a picnic thrown in; anything to escape school for a few hours. Oh, the halcyon days of youth! Endless summer evenings and a packet of five Woodbines tucked safely down our regulation bloomers.

What made me wander off I cannot recall. Perhaps we were playing hide and seek, but I found myself in a small wood, completely alone. Something drew me further into this silent world, away from the giggles and the laughter. The voices, now faint, were like a memory. On I went in the complete stillness. And there in front of me I saw my seductress. At the foot of a silver birch, growing out of vivid green moss, was a simple primrose. Not a dead leaf or bloom to spoil its flawlessness; it was all fresh growth and expectation.

Mindful lest I disregard such perfection, the sun sent a shaft of light blazing down through the trees. As surely as I had seen a spotlight pick out the good fairy in a pantomime did the beam engulf the primrose. Had Titania herself emerged from those fragile petals, it could not have enchanted me more.

For a moment, time stood still and all the silliness of youth fell away.

🖉 🖉 🖉

While we would never pick an orchid, we were positively encouraged to pick wild flowers. Nowadays it is not permissible, but we never plundered, simply picked a specimen here or there. When we returned to school Miss Cobbley would help us to identify them. She encouraged us to look the names up ourselves and then they were placed individually, never mixed, in toothbrush mugs above the sinks where we cleaned our teeth after meals. Looking back, during the summer months the mugs were always in use: Speedwell, ground ivy, lesser bug wort, daisy . . . I can see them now. In our very best handwriting, we would write out the common name, followed by the Latin, on a card and place it beside the flower. It was one of the school activities that I positively enjoyed, but of course I forgot about it the moment I left.

That is, until I had children of my own. Young children have a habit of picking one flower or one blade of grass at a time. They seem to lack the urge, unlike adults, to pick copious amounts of the same thing. Instead they seem to prefer, say, just one dandelion and study it with the genuine wonderment of youth. It's all too easy to throw away a single stem either during a ramble or on returning home. Many's the time I've been caught out by one of the children with, 'Where's that flower I gave you?' I blush to remember how readily I discarded it.

Then I had an idea. Outside the kitchen door is an old wooden table where things are randomly dumped on the return from a walk. Memories of Miss Cobbley and school were stirred and gradually we developed what was to become the 'interest table'. I encourage the children to identify their finds for themselves as we had once done.

It has added another dimension to our walks. The children are now on a constant quest for treasures to take home.

While the table was originally intended for all things natural, sometimes an inanimate object has taken pride of place. Flotsam along the tide line is a rich source of finds. With lots of encouragement, the children are now beginning to use books for reference as they vie with each other in their haste to identify feathers shells or leaves. Joe comes into the kitchen with a huge chrysalis in his hand. I know it is an elephant hawk moth, but preferring him to name it himself, I say, 'I've got a book about it somewhere.'

'I'm going to put that on your gravestone,' he says.

'Put what, Joe?' I ask.

'You always say that, whatever we talk about. You've got a book about it somewhere.'

Joe, in fact, has invented his own, very singular, way of categorising nature. His criterion for judging small things is whether they could eat a frog or whether a frog could eat them.

On one occasion I find Dan sitting at the back door poring over a book called *A Hand Guide to the Sea Coast*. In front of him is a pile of objects gleaned from an early morning walk. Among the old fishing hooks, tangled line, stones and shells, he picks up a discarded condom and waving it at me says, 'I can't find this anywhere in the book.'

Or, in the middle of tea, Elfie suddenly decides she wanted to get some tadpoles. So once we have finished we jump on our bikes, complete with nets and buckets, and set off to the heath. It is only a couple of miles away and when we arrive it is quite deserted; a lovely, still fine evening. We only manage to catch four tadpoles but with various pieces of weeds, a snail and some water boatmen insects, the children are delighted. It is almost dark when we arrive home, so there is no time for proper homework. Instead Dan and I construct an aquarium for our new acquisitions while Elfie finds a book and identifies the weeds. It is one of the joys of living here: whichever direction we choose there are always marvellous walks or rides.

A magical evening. Although sadly, much of the time Elfie is now more intrigued by *Neighbours* than pond dipping.

Never contrived, the interest table has simply evolved a life, a momentum of its own, as it follows the seasons. And more than one artist friend has commented on our 'still life' at the back door.

Chapter 27

Toads

'Good afternoon listeners, this is John Eley and you are listening to "Country Matters" at Radio Suffolk. Today we have in the studio the Toad Lady of Dunwich.'

I do wish he'd stop calling me that. I mean I'm fond of toads but . . . really.

'Now Nicky, if you could begin by telling the listeners how this whole project began.'

'Hi,' I say more nervously than I could have imagined. My hands are clammy, my throat dry.

John winks at me encouragingly.

'It was quite simple really. I was walking the children to the school bus one morning and we noticed a squashed toad on the road. Then within a distance of about two hundred yards, we counted another twenty. Dead ones! It was a horrible!'

'And when was this?'

'A couple of months ago.'

'Then what . . . tell us . . . what did you do?' says John, gesticulating with his hand in what I can only presume is an attempt to get me to lighten up a bit.

'As we waited for the bus, we decided to find out every
thing we could about toads. We knew so little. When I got
home I phoned the Suffolk Wildlife Trust. They were really
helpful and gave me the name of a chap at the Herpetofauna
Society.'

'The what?'

'No, I hadn't heard of it either; they major in all things
reptilian. Anyway they sent us loads of literature. The children, Elfie and Dan, came home from school bursting with
facts. We learnt that during the winter the toad hibernates,
emerging in the spring for the mating season. This can be
any time between February and March depending on the
weather . . .'

'Do go on.'

'Are you sure . . . I'm not banging on . . . am I?'

'Of course not, our listeners will be fascinated.'

'Anyway, we wanted to do something about it.'

'Like what exactly?'

'Firstly we painted and erected two signs to alert people
to watch out for toads. Then we galvanised friends with
children, people in the village, to help with a nightly patrol.'

'Patrol to do what?'

'To pick the toads up. You see, they migrate back to the
pond, ditch or wherever it was they were spawned. Mostly
at dusk. Often this involves crossing roads and that's when
they're run over. So the idea was to carry them, preferably in
the direction they were heading.'

'You mean you actually picked them up? Isn't that rather
disgusting, they're all slimy, aren't they?'

'No, this is what really annoys me, they're not slimy, but
being cold-blooded they are cold to the touch. People have
completely the wrong idea about toads; they think they're

venomous, if they pee on you you'll gets warts, all sorts of stupid stuff. Anyway they're not peeing; it's just some acrid liquid to scare predators. It's all complete balls and makes me so cross!'

'Nicky, would you mind your language. We are going out live.'

'Sorry! But you know, I'm now beginning to define my friends: those who like toads and those who don't!'

'Okay, go on, you were telling the listeners about your patrol.'

'From dusk onwards, we walked up and down the road with torches and a bucket and carried them across. It sounds a bit obvious, but it's important to take them in the direction they're heading. Can I just say that children must be accompanied by an adult. Wouldn't be much good if you saved a toad only to have your child squashed.' I giggle nervously.

'Piece of good advice there. Anyway how many do you reckon you saved?'

'About a hundred.'

'So not many then?'

'Not many! You sound like the man from the council office.'

'What do you mean?'

'I'll tell you what I mean,' I say, warming up. 'We were told by Suffolk Wildlife that the council would erect proper signs for us, you know, a big red triangle with a picture of a toad in the middle. By the way, some bastard pinched the ones the kids made. I rang them up . . . the council . . . not the bastard. They said yes of course we could have two *if* we could prove Dunwich was a migration route. So I said what sort of proof. And do you know what he said? He only wanted me to collect a thousand dead toads as evidence. So I said . . .'

'I think it's better if you don't tell us what you said. I am beginning to get your drift,' he says hurriedly.

'I'm sorry but it all makes me so cross. I mean really, if we had to wait to collect that many there would be no toads left. That's when we decided to hold a sale of work to raise the money for the signs ourselves. Actually, the parish offered to pay, but I'd got the bit between my teeth; far better for the children to raise the money themselves.'

'So you had a toad sale, how very original. What did you do?'

'Yes. Everyone was completely marvellous. My mother painted cards. The boys made dear little Fymo models of amphibians holding placards saying *Down with cars* . . . I did mention that I picked up two newts outside the pub . . . didn't I? Then there were the squashed toad biscuits, they were the highlight of the sale.'

'The what?'

'It was quite funny, well not at the time it wasn't. Elfie and I baked hundreds of biscuits, then she iced a bright green toad on each one. The table was covered in them when Dan came in with a Dinky tractor which he started pushing all over the biscuits. Hell broke out, you know what kids are like? But when I looked at the damage, they looked like squashed toads, like they'd been run over, well I suppose they had really. Brilliant. They were a complete sell-out.'

'So the sale was a success then? I know it was reported in the local press; that's how my researcher heard of you and rang you up.'

'Gosh, yes . . . I really must apologise for telling her to piss off. When she phoned and asked me to talk on the radio, I genuinely thought it was a friend winding me up.'

'Language!'

'Yes, the sale was a success. We raised more than we needed for the signs. People were really generous.'

'Well Nicky, just before we come to the end, we've had a call from one of our listeners. She is longing to know why St James's Street in Dunwich was closed for a week.'

'You said you wouldn't mention that,' I said, blushing.

'I know, but now we're on air it's too good a story to miss. Come on, tell us.'

'OK then. You know in the movies the police always draw an outline around a corpse on the road?' I began.

'Yes . . .'

'Well I had this brainwave. On the morning of the sale I got up at first light and painted circles round all the tiny bodies of the squashed toads. I thought it would be really effective for showing the public the extent of the carnage. People were fascinated when I pointed them out. I'm sure it raised their awareness, which after all was what the whole thing was in aid of. It worked really well.'

'Until Monday, that is?' says John with a smirk.

'Do I really have to say any more?' By this time I could really clock him one.

'Yes, please Nicky. Do tell our listeners.'

'I wasn't to know there was a pipe leak under the road.'

'Go on.'

'On the Monday after the sale, these men from Anglia Water arrived in St James's Street. You know how early they start. Well bugger me if they didn't think that my little circles were where they were meant to drill!'

'And do tell us, how many circles did you paint?'

'To be honest I'm not sure, I mean not that many. But I suppose there were several . . .'

Chapter 28

A Square Peg

I have an abiding impression that my mother's education was not to her liking. I believe her artistic parents treated schooling in an altogether cursory fashion and minded little as to its outcome. That Mum's grammar and numeracy was always superior to my sister's and mine owes more to the period in which she was schooled, not to mention her applied diligence, than her parents' intervention.

It was inevitable, therefore, when she found herself in a position where she could afford to choose for her own daughters, she chose private. There was ever the assumption that if it cost a lot it must be better. But I cannot deny I always felt her choice was influenced not so much by what would suit us as individuals, but what she herself would have wished.

As I have already mentioned, siblings may differ; and we did.

Ironically the school she chose for us put very little store on learning. And while I galloped through boarding school with a gang of like-minded anarchists known affectionately as the Banana Bunch, my sister hated it with the same degree of passion as I loved it.

No one seemed to mind that we left school with the minimum of exams; it had cost a fortune and that sufficed.

There then followed one of the most absurd periods of my life. I was sent away to finishing school. If you look up *finishing* in the dictionary you will read: to complete, the making of, the last touch; that makes a perfect job. I shall start at the end, by expanding on my expulsion.

✐ I received a message to go directly to Mrs Dickie's office. Now, given she was the headmistress, I was always intrigued that her bedroom doubled as her study. Admittedly the bed was always made and covered with a rich velvet patchwork cover but it was still more a bedroom than an office.

I knocked on the familiar oak door and waited for her command.

'Come in,' she called gently.

'Oh there you are Nicky, thank you for coming so promptly. Now take a seat, there's something I have to talk to you about.'

I really liked Mrs Dickie. She was a thoroughly decent human being and always struck me as being genuinely fair. So there was absolutely nothing I could say to defend myself when she proceeded to say:

'As you may well be aware, Winkfield has no equal when it comes to finishing schools, and we are justly proud of our reputation. The waiting list for entrants is some years long. Indeed,' and here she referred to a piece of paper on her desk, 'indeed your mother put you and your sister down on the entrants list over ten years ago when you were only seven. So you see how special it is,' she said.

I looked at the rich velvet patchwork cover on her bed and wondered how long it would have taken someone to make.

'Are you listening to me, Nicky?'

'Yes,' I smiled while wondering where all this was going. I had heard it several times already from my mother.

'I have just been on the phone to your parents; we would like you to leave at the end of this term.' Here she had the good grace to pause so that I might take in what she had just said. Then she continued, 'And they are in total agreement with what I am about to say.'

'I'm sorry. I don't understand,' I said.

'Nicky, we like you well enough. You are popular with both teachers and fellow students, but really my dear, that is not enough now, is it? Quite frankly you are a square peg in a round hole and as such you will save our time and your parents' money if you leave at the end of the summer.'

Ostensibly we were here to learn cookery, dressmaking, including trimming hats and glove making, secretarial skills, deportment and any other life skills that might enable us to ensnare a rich husband. When I suggested if he was that rich, there would be no need to know how to iron a shirt properly, I was told not to be so insolent.

I simply thought it was based on a wrong set of principles. It was inevitable that I should question it.

I have a daughter of my own. I remember what it was like to be seventeen with all the accompanying hormonally confusing messages. Now who, in the name of all that is gracious, would deem it appropriate to incarcerate her in an institution and spend a whole term, a whole term, learning how to make white or béchamel sauce, and the variations thereof; cauliflower cheese, soufflés, Sauce Anglaise and so on? Certainly not me.

Then there were the days spent pulling carnations to bits. Petal by petal we would dismantle a perfectly adequate bloom, laying them in a circle in the order in which they had been removed. Then we were shown how to meticulously wire each one and painstakingly reassemble them into their previous form. And the reasoning behind such mindless destruction was simple: to remove the offending lumpy bit at the back of the poor flower so that it would lie flat on a lapel and make the perfect buttonhole. PLEASE!

We learnt how to light a cigarette elegantly, how to enter a room and turn heads, how to get in and out of a sports car without showing too much of our knickers. Happily there were also wine tastings where some of us swilled but omitted to spit the wine out afterwards. Our social assets burgeoned and were too numerous to count.

But there wasn't a great deal I was going to miss and I was not sorry to be leaving. But in fairness to Mrs Dickie, and finishing school, I had never been expelled with so much grace before.

🌢 🌢 🌢

My sister's experience of finishing school was the complete antithesis of mine. The course was for three terms; I was asked to leave halfway through my second. If they deemed you had the potential, you were 'invited' to return for a fourth term and take your Cordon Bleu exam. Thankfully, if only for Mum's sake, Terry got the selector's nod and became the star turn. And unlike me she has turned all she learnt to great advantage.

My sister and her husband John now run a splendid old country house hotel in Devon. While John deals with front

Chapter 29

Quails

The April child wants quails. Given the singularity of such a request, I feel he must be indulged. From where the notion came, heaven alone knows, but as he is the youngest and rarely asks for anything, I cannot deny this simple demand.

Where, I wonder, do you buy quails? With infinite patience and a deal of sleuthing, I find myself packing the children into the car and heading for a housing estate in Ipswich. After numerous wrong turns, I pull up in front of the neatest bungalow imaginable. Surely I have the wrong address. Were I in search of crocheted dolls to camouflage loo-rolls I would be more certain, but quails? I'm not convinced. However, a knock at the door confirms that we have indeed found the right place. Mrs Quail is immaculate; not at all what I envisaged: blue-rinsed, tightly permed hair, twin-set, pearls and a smart little tweed skirt. But why I should presume that quail breeding be the sole province of the scruffy and muddy is my problem. Only her hands and her footwear belies the fact that she actually spends most of her time in the great outdoors, eschewing the crochet hook.

We follow Mrs Quail into an extremely pretty back garden and make our way towards four large sheds at the bottom. All the while she twitters away about the joys of these tiny birds. Originally from Japan, they were initially kept for their song. It seems they mature in six weeks and the female can lay up to three hundred eggs in her short life. I confirm that we want five hens and a cock bird. Collecting a small cardboard box, Mrs Quail carefully leads us into a shed where I get my first glimpse of these minute birds. She stoops, catches one and then rather unceremoniously sticks her index finger up its backside. Catching my expression she imparts another snippet of quail management. If it's a female, your finger will fit neatly between the bones in its bottom, the space for an egg to pass; the chaps, however, have very little space, for obvious reasons. It is also an indicator as to whether or not they are in lay. As they all look identical, this little pearl has proved invaluable.

Deary me, but quails are very small! Some sage assured us they would live happily in an old rabbit run. What the sage omitted to divulge was their facility for flight. The distance between cardboard box and run is minimal but sufficient to lose fifty per cent of our purchase before we have time to close the cage door. Off they go, winging their way out across the marshes, our raucous yelling and flapping of arms proving completely ineffectual. However, there is an egg, albeit the tiniest, at the bottom of the box. Compensation for loss I muse, while clinging to the naive belief that the escapologists will feel lonely and wish to return to the cosy environs their siblings were now enjoying. I do not at that juncture realise that quail are closely related to partridge and as such are more wild than domesticated. Fool! But then, how much quail lore is it possible, or perhaps healthy, for one person to acquire in a day?

For the time being we content ourselves with the ones we have left, in the knowledge that quail mature quickly. Rapidly our three burgeon into dozens. Baby quail resemble nothing so much as bumblebees, and are quite charming.

Before long, Joe has turned entrepreneur and is selling baskets of speckled eggs, complete with cooking instructions, at the gate. *Boil gently for 3 minutes, drain and allow to cool in cold water. The shells are so pretty, serve them unpeeled; 4–6 per person in a nest of finely shredded lettuce with a small dish of celery salt.*

Meanwhile I, with my newly acquired sexing skills, surreptitiously remove and dispatch the surfeit of males.

Raising three spirited children necessitates some house rules. One such rule is to at least taste what I put in front of them at the table. I concede they will not always like everything I proffer, but what they are not allowed to do is grimace, say, 'Ugh, that's puke! How could anyone eat that?', pull a face and spit it out. I explain it is most offputting to others, especially those in the throes of enjoying said dish.

One weekend, with friends staying, I choose roast partridge for dinner. As an added treat, the children are to stay up and join us. In a moment of sheer inspiration, how delightful, I think, to serve each child with its diminutive cousin; the partridge's cousin that is.

Imagine the scene: candles flickering and flattering the glowing faces. I dish up a partridge for each adult and a perfect little roast quail for each child. It does look completely designer even if I say so myself. As I place the bowl of potatoes on the table, I pretend not to hear the first rumblings of dissent from below the salt.

'What's this?'

'What have we got?'

'Is it a baby partridge?'

Me: 'Not really. Just try it, see what you think. How many spuds do you want?'

'Oh yuk! It's a toad. Look, I've taken the bacon off. It's a toad!'

'Don't be so silly. Of course it's not.'

'Well what is it then?'

'Anyone for gravy?' I ask.

'I'm not even trying mine, so there.'

The mutterings persisted as I feign the gracious hostess. 'Now come on you lot, you know the rules.'

'No, this is well out of order,' one of the children continues. 'That's it! All you've done is cut off their feet so we wouldn't guess.'

I glance in the direction of the voice. The April child is carefully dissecting the carcass on his plate. It hadn't dawned on me what an imaginative child might think I had served up; equally I lack the heart to admit my crime. How could I?

'Mine's got a wishbone. It can't be an amphibian. I know exactly what it is. It's a quail! Isn't it? That's completely rank! It's even worse than I thought.'

With that, the children rise as one. They are not interested in my protestations.

'What are you supposed to do with an excess of males?' I call after them. But they are not of a mind to listen. Like a flock of little birds, they are off, and with them any vestige of my hard-earned authority.

Not wishing to be outdone by his younger brother's entrepreneurial skills in the egg department, Dan says he'd like to do a paper round. I think it's a terrific idea and am delighted at the budding initiative in one of such tender years.

I mention it to the owner of our local village shop some three miles away. What I fail to register is the eagerness with which he jumps at the opportunity to offload this chore onto an unsuspecting mum. I say mum, for it is not until we have taken it on that I realise that the legal age for a paper round is thirteen. I should wish.

'How old is your son?' he asks.

'Eleven,' I tell him.

'Well, we'll have to put your name on the computer then.'

'That's fine,' I say. 'When shall we start?'

'As soon as you can. If you could pick the papers up from here about six-thirty, I'll have them sorted and named so all you have to do is deliver them.'

I thank him heartily and as I turn to leave the shop, I notice an assistant removing a sign from the window, which reads . . . 'WANTED . . . PAPER PEOPLE. Would suit OAP'. Oh no it wouldn't.

So now I find myself jumping out of bed, pulling on the first clothes I can lay my hands on and driving off to collect the papers. In fairness Dan is dressed and waiting by the time I return, but invariably the sun isn't actually in the sky at such an hour. Our little village is very spread out and I can't possibly have him crossing roads in the dark. So I leave him to do 'the street', while I end up doing the lion's share.

If I don't get collared by someone for a chat or an errand I may just be back in time to take the children to the school bus. On a positive note, sometimes when I used to wake and lay in bed I was given to dark thoughts. There is no time for that now. I'm up and running before they have a chance to kick in.

Chapter 30

A Lesson

My children are not given to always expecting brand new things. They are quite used to hand-me-downs. However, Dan has reached that self-conscious age when he would prefer not to be seen on his sister's old bike.

As he had been excelling on the school front, I felt a brand new BMX was in order. It is wonderful to see how much pleasure this gives him, until one afternoon he comes into the kitchen and asks, 'Have you seen my bike?'

'No, why?' I reply. 'Where did you leave it?'

'I think by the front gate, but I can't find it anywhere. Joe!' he shouts, 'have you moved my bike?'

After an abortive search we concede that it has been stolen.

'Darling . . . you do know this is your fault for being so careless,' I say.

'That's not fair, it's the person who nicked it's fault,' he protests.

I'm not sure I agree with that . . .

✎ Years ago I au paired in Italy. As jobs go it was fairly laid-back. I was paid in a casual sort of a way when my boss either remembered or had the money about him.

Anyway, the family belonged to a lido or swimming club on the banks of Lake Varese. I would take the children there almost daily so they could swim near the safety of lifeguards and use the shower facilities afterwards. There were also the usual cafes and ball games. Most of the members were English but there was the odd Italian family and it was all very genteel.

On this particular day I had been paid for the last two months. In Italian lira this was a vast amount of money, a real wodge of notes; thousands and thousands of lira, which in reality amounted to about £30. Nonetheless it was my wages along with my keep. On the way to the lido I bought a page of stamps that I tucked inside the notes and bunged into my bag.

There was a communal changing room where we slipped into our costumes and left our belongings.

We were lounging in the sun when Mary, my employer, asked if she might borrow a stamp. Back in the changing room I opened my bag but couldn't find the stamps or the money. I was not unduly concerned, simply thought I must have mislaid it. I returned to Mary and said that I couldn't find the stamps. We gave it no more thought.

As we lay in the heat we became increasingly aware of activity. I noticed one of the lifeguards locking the iron gates and sensed an air of tension amongst some of the staff. Within minutes we heard raised voices and to our horror saw one of our 'friends' being escorted by two burly lifeguards. My Italian was not my strong point but it was evident we were witnessing some kind of arrest.

We heard the sound of a police car, then the gates were

opened to let in what I can only imagine were plain-clothed policemen.

After some minutes one of them approached me and asked me to go with him into the changing room. There to my horror was this girl – a girl I not only knew but regarded as a friend, sitting on a bench sobbing her heart out. She was flanked by men who were treating her rather roughly. They were prodding her, goading her and calling her things in a language I could not understand, although I definitely got the thrust of what they were saying. She was being accused of theft.

One of the officers approached me; in his hand was a wodge of notes. 'Is this your money?' he asked in Italian. I could understand this much.

As I said, thirty pounds to me was a deal of money, but it was the sort of amount that many affluent and not so affluent members of a private club could have about them.

I shrugged my shoulders and said I didn't know.

'What do you mean you don't know? You were overheard saying you thought you had lost money.'

I thought back to my conversation with Mary. We obviously had been overheard.

The stamps! Of course, the stamps. I'd tucked them into the middle of the money.

I turned to the officer and said in the best Italian I could muster, 'It may be my money, I can't be certain. But if it is mine there will be a sheet of stamps tucked in the middle.'

He looked at me quizzically.

All the while the girl sat on the bench sobbing. I smiled at her reassuringly.

The officer handed me the money and I took it. I leafed through the big papery notes, once, twice, three times – there were no stamps.

The men stared at me aghast. 'It's your money. You've got your money back. Why are you worrying about a few stamps?'

I tried to explain it wasn't the value of the stamps, it was merely a way of substantiating whether or not it was mine. It wasn't working. My Italian didn't stretch to such subtleties. I asked if Mary might join us since her Italian was perfect.

I told her my side of the story, then listened to their version. They spoke so quickly I could grasp little. As they gesticulated to the sobbing figure in the corner, it became apparent that she was being accused. I couldn't believe it. I knew her; she was seemingly wealthy. She'd taken me out for lunch the previous week and insisted on paying for it. There must be some mistake.

Mary took my arm and we went outside.

'Sit down,' she said. 'It appears things have been missing for weeks. People have been reporting suspected thefts. So much so those two new lifeguards are in fact detectives. One of them overheard you mentioning the stamps. They immediately closed the gates and arrested Maria.'

'But why her?'

'They've suspected her for some time. They simply had to wait till they caught her red-handed, which of course is what's happened.'

'I don't believe it. She's really sweet. Ask them again about the stamps. You see if they aren't on her, or with the money, it can't be her can it?'

I watched Mary trying to explain my theory. The detective looked up and gave me a withering look. He shook his head.

'There are no stamps, but he thinks you're being petty. Feels you should be grateful that you got your money back. They've arrested Maria; they're taking her down to the police station.'

'They want us to join them – to make a statement.'

When we arrived we were told Maria had been charged with theft and would be tried within the month.

Mary and the detective were deep in conversation. He kept glancing in my direction. I felt physically sick.

'Come over here,' said Mary. 'The inspector has something to say to you.'

'You realise that you are partly to blame for this. It is deeply disturbing for me because she is the daughter of my superior. She has her problems, weight being one of them; and very low self-esteem. I'm no psychologist but I believe she felt she could buy friendships.'

I thought of her generosity.

'But why am I to blame?' I asked.

'We have responsibility to others. If you hadn't left temptation in her way she couldn't have stolen it. So you see it's partly your fault.'

This is something I have never forgotten. If I don't want something nicked, I look after it.

✍ ✍ ✍

Chapter 31

Fowlplay

I do so miss living and sharing my life with a kindred spirit. There is so much I have done on my own and enjoyed, but I would be kidding myself if I said I was totally happy. On good days I wonder if I will ever love again. I really don't think I trust love or men. I'd much rather get on with things my own way. One thing is certain, I would find it much more difficult to write and pursue my own dreams with a man, however wonderful, waiting in the wings. But I equally hope I am not bitter or will ever become so.

And then I go for a walk and find myself thinking again: blustery violent sea, not a soul about. This would be the most wonderful place to have an affair. But only in the winter, when it is so special . . . long walks, cosy lunches at the pub, big roaring fires. I start to think of the type of man I could possibly tolerate now. Married men are off limits. Divorced? I would wonder whose fault it might have been. Widowed? Would set me off as well . . . It all seems too impossible to dwell on. On balance I'd rather have the children and my integrity.

But enough of such thoughts; I've promised the boys a works outing!

I am taking them to our local bird reserve. Joe in particular is now obsessed with the natural world. Anything that can be bunged in a jam jar or pushed under a microscope is fair game. Well, as it's half term I have booked us into a bird-watching day at Minsmere. But how, I ponder, have I managed to spawn an embryonic twitcher? It rather worries me: the other day I caught Joe in the pantry, not in pursuit of provisions for a midnight feast, like any normal red-blooded child. He was pretending it was a hide, peering out through the tiny window, identifying birds in the garden! It was all rather disturbing. But I have resolved to waive any mistrust of this species of humanity, along with their sartorial idiosyncrasies, in favour of my maternal instinct.

'Autumn Migrants' is the theme of the day. To set the scene, and by way of lending more of an air of adventure, we arrive on our bikes. Given the cold easterly winds howling in from the North Sea, I am expecting the day will be one to be endured rather than enjoyed. My heart sinks as we arrive in the car park: cagoules, anoraks and binoculars abound. The chap leading our group is called Frank. At first he seems somewhat uninspiring.

After a brief introduction to the reserve, he shows us in mind-numbing detail the correct way to use binoculars or 'bins', as I now believe the more hardened twitchers call them. And what a bunch they are. Off we go at a spanking pace towards 'the scrape'. This he explains, between enthusiastic sightings of our more elusive autumn visitors, is a man-made habitat specifically designed to attract wading birds.

Choughs and tits feature largely in the talk, all without a

hint of irony. I resolve to be less puerile but humour, I note, is about as elusive as a shag. Joe's hand is clutching mine and he is beaming with anticipation, so I attempt to curb any sarcastic thoughts. Who in the name of all that is gracious wants to spend their days trudging around a bird reserve identifying thirteen types of tits? And no, I am not being salacious. There are, I now know, marsh, reed, willow, long-tailed and on and on . . .

Cold air always makes me yawn and I am miles away when Frank asks if I have understood what he has been saying. I realise how rude I must appear and feel chastened, but not in an altogether unpleasant way. I try to pull myself together. This is, after all, the boys' day and surely I can make some semblance of enjoying it.

After what feels like an age, we reach North Hide. We all pile in, with me as ever bringing up the rear. All the seats are taken but Frank immediately stands up and gives me his. It is then that I notice how very shy he is. Despite his gentle smile, he constantly averts his gaze and avoids any eye contact.

Ahead of us is a vast expanse of water, some small islandy bits and, amazingly, flocks of wading birds. Judging by the 'ahs', 'oohs' and 'over there's' our fellow twitchers are in their element. Joe is fumbling with his 'bins' but Frank notices and immediately goes over to help him. I am too far away to hear what he is saying, but I do notice the ease with which he points out birds and helps the boys to identify them.

As we walk back towards Island Mere, Frank stops and picks something up. He tries to hand it to me, but frankly it looks rather disgusting so I shake my head. Then he gropes in his pocket and tips the contents onto a table. Honestly, it reminds me of *Just William*: string, penknife, little bits of this and that. Then he pulls out a Petri dish containing bits of an owl pellet; a tawny owl to be precise. He points out some tiny little bones – 'a shrew!' he tells us excitedly. Well! That does it for me: his innocence, his childlike enthusiasm, his palpable joy in such simple things.

On our walk back he waxes lyrical about something called succession, how oak forest is the natural vegetation of these isles and as such they sustain over 300 sub-species, from insects to mammals. He even opens up an oak apple and shows us the wasp grub inside. Very nutritious as survival food, he tells us. Oh goodness! I could run on for pages.

The man has fired me up, me who was so jaundiced by life and men in particular; fired up, but not by some hunk with a fast car and an oversized ego, but a vague, absent-minded, old-fashioned gentleman. One who could no more make a cheap jibe than shoot an avocet.

I am walking on air. The moon is brighter, the day more exciting, all because of him. I know nothing will come of it, and why should it? It honestly doesn't matter. What does is the way he has inspired me, opened my eyes to the fact that there are still decent, charming people out there; people with real values for a change.

I almost feel he has renewed my faith in men; I am in love with life again and for that I will be eternally grateful.

I have just booked us all in for an evening walk. We are to listen to nightjars and if we are extremely lucky we may just get a glimpse of glow-worms! Already I am looking at things in a different light.

And then, it is a friend's birthday one weekend and we all go to the pub. An old acquaintance arrives with rather an interesting man. I, as ever, pretend I haven't noticed him. But, I shall have to do a little homework on that one, I think.

Chapter 32

Cottage Teas

Once again the boring old chestnut of earning money is rearing its head. As ever, my main priority is to be at home for the children when they need me, so this precludes 'going out to work', especially as the summer holidays are almost upon us.

I am returning from a soulful walk along the beach, wondering how I could make a quantum leap forward with my finances when I recognise Mary's car outside the cottage.

Mary is one of my friends who inspired the dream. When we first met she was travelling about East Anglia living in a horse-drawn wagon, following the work and the seasons. We share endless happy memories of innocent, carefree days.

After huge bear hugs and initial niceties, we progress into the kitchen where I put the kettle on. As we wait for the water to boil we exchange the usual good-natured banter and catch up with each other's lives. It appears from what she is telling me that her monetary assets are equally becalmed.

We take our mugs of coffee into the front garden and sit on the bench beneath the towering hollyhocks. It is a particularly handsome day and the garden looks good. I have allowed the shrubs at the front of the garden to grow up and now they are big enough to shield us from the road and more importantly, prying eyes. A tiny wren darts in and out of the roof in the front porch while a pair of goldfinches, or King Harrys as they are known about here, busy themselves in the variegated holly. It is almost overly pretty, it is so perfect.

As we drink our coffee we go through the usual liturgy of ideas; listing our assets or accomplishments. Donkey rides on the beach, not enough money, too slow. Mary has a horse not unlike Doris and we moot giving cart rides around the village. That seems not only fun but could be quite an earner, until I remember it would necessitate me leaving Joe, who is still too young to be left on his own. There is also the spectre of one of the horses bolting with a cartload of tourists.

'No, it's no good. It's got to be something I can do from here,' I say, waving both my arms about. 'That's it! From here! Why didn't I think about it before?'

'What do you mean?' says Mary.

'Look at this garden! It's a typical cottage garden; well, it is if we put Bun in the back garden and tidy it up a bit,' I continue. 'Get rid of all the kids' stuff.'

'I still don't know what you're getting at,' says Mary.

'Teas!' I say. 'Cream teas.'

'Teas?' says Mary, screwing up her face and looking at me as if I'd lost it.

'Yes, teas. Think about it . . . there's a pub up the road but there's nowhere for all the visitors to have a good old-fashioned cream tea.'

'Do you mean here?' asks Mary.

'Absolutely, here! It's ideal. If we just use the front garden then the children can still play in the back out of sight. It'll be perfect,' I say, getting into my stride. 'Look, think about it, we're both very good cooks if we keep it simple.'

'But we'll need chairs and tables and all sorts of things,' says Mary.

'I know that! But come on though, in principle, are you up for it?'

'Absolutely!'

The rest of the morning we spend drawing up a plan. We make 'to do' and 'to buy' lists, and by lunchtime our new venture is only days away from realisation.

Our idea is to use only the front garden; to find or buy enough tables and chairs to seat a maximum of, say, twenty-four. Mary is to make flowery tablecloths while I blitz the kitchen and bring it up to speed. There is a factory shop nearby that sells china seconds and by the end of the week we have purchased all we could need to serve a quintessential afternoon tea to twenty-four people simultaneously. So convinced are we that this will prove irresistible we make contingency plans in the event of a rush.

It is three weeks until the summer holidays; a time when we shall capitalise on the influx of tourists that swarm about these parts. By way of a little practice we decide to open on Saturdays and Sundays up to the holidays and after that perhaps four days a week to see how it goes.

The menu is simple, and with only six tables we handwrite them:

Pot of tea
Coffee
Sandwiches (cucumber, cheese or tuna)
Cream tea
Scones
Clotted cream and homemade jam
Variety of homemade cakes

Mary's a dab hand at scones; just as well really, for although I know I'm a good cook, pastry and scones remain a mystery to me. But my chocolate cake is terrific. So all in all, the division of labour is fairly straightforward. By the following weekend our new venture is launched.

Like me, Mary has many more hidden strings to her bow; she is actually a signwriter by trade. On Saturday morning she arrives early and together we put up the tables and generally knock the place into some semblance of order. My main contribution has been to bring the kitchen up to a standard worthy of catering; I think if nothing else comes of this new venture, I shall at least have a clean kitchen after all these years.

Not only has Mary made the flowery tablecloths but now I find we are to wear matching aprons sewn from the remainder of the material. Lastly she tells me to close my eyes and stretch out my hands. I do as I am told and when I open them, there before me is a magnificent hand-painted sign to advertise our wares. And so it is, at two o'clock on a sunny June afternoon, we duly plonk a gaily painted blackboard, emblazoned with . . .

Cottage Teas
OPEN

in the middle of the pavement and patiently await our first punters.

I do it every time, every single time; and I never seem to learn. It was the same when I first put up a sign for *Goats' milk*. I spent the previous evening worrying how I would possibly cope with the demand. Then Joe's *Quails' eggs* . . . it was weeks before the public realised what they had been missing. My enthusiasm always runs away with me.

But slowly, too slowly really, the word spreads and our little enterprise begins to take off. For the most part the children keep a low profile but there are inevitably occasions when my attention is divided.

'Puss has had something really interesting on the landing,' says Joe with a degree of urgency. 'Will you come and have a look?'

I'm in the middle of serving tea to a family of four. 'Hang on a mo,' I say.

'Let me just see to this table and I'll be right there.' No sooner have I finished when I follow Joe up the stairs, wiping sticky fingers down my floral pinnie.

There, on the green carpet, just outside his bedroom door are two little dark red spheres. I bend down to scrutinise them more closely.

'I haven't a clue what it could be,' I say in complete honesty.

As I say this I notice the cage door to the Russian hamsters is ajar.

'Where are the hamsters? You were playing with them in your castles the last time I saw them; they were running along the battlements. You did put them away didn't you?'

A little speckled face stares up at me, pondering.

'Darling, tell me, you did put them away, didn't you?'

'I can't remember.'

We both turn and inspect what was on the floor once more.

'I hate to tell you, but I think Puss has eaten them. Those are their little balls, and I think that looks like a tiny liver,' I say, prodding another, what I now strongly suspect are hamster body parts.

Joe breaks into a rage and goes in search of the cat.

I clear up the mess and return to my guests. They are seated at table with a gaily checked tablecloth sipping tea and extolling the prettiness of my garden. My heart swells with pride.

'What a completely lovely cottage you have. It's idyllic, so peaceful,' says the good lady of the family.

As if on cue, no sooner has the word 'peaceful' passed her lips when Puss comes catapulting out of the bedroom window immediately above them.

He lands, fortunately the right way up, in the middle of their table, sending creams teas complete with extra jam over the seated guests.

I am not sure as to who is more surprised. Puss, however, is the first to compose himself and, after a cursory shaking, begins to *faire* his *toilette*. He sits right in the middle of the table licking cream from his paws.

Suddenly the front door opens and Dan and Joe rush out brandishing lightsabers. 'There he is,' they shout, as they charge toward the cat, completely regardless of my paying guests.

It's August Bank Holiday weekend and with the weather set to be a scorcher, we anticipate brisk trade. While on Saturday business is much the same as usual, by two-thirty on the Sunday the punters are already piling in. Mary is plating up some scones while I carry a tray of homemade lemonade out to a young family sitting in the shade. I look up and see another two families cross the lawn.

'Gosh Mary, I think we're going to need a hand. Shall we ask the girls?'

Amber, Mary's daughter, is staying so I call her and Elfie through from the sitting room where they had been watching telly.

'Do you fancy doing a spot of waitressing, darlings? We're so pushed. Look at all these people.'

After the initial, 'Do we have to?', I say there'll be money in it and to just go and get ready – and quickly.

Mary and I are tearing about clearing tables, making tuna sandwiches and whipping cream, when I yell up the stairs to the girls to get a move on.

'We're just changing,' comes the reply.

'No need, you were fine in your jeans,' I shout, desperate for them to just shake a leg and get down here.

I am clearing a table ready for the next couple who are waiting patiently when I catch the expression on the husband's face. I turn around and there tottering across the garden is my teenage daughter and her friend in hotpants, high-heeled shoes and covered in make-up, looking like a couple of tarts.

Then there was the day when I overheard a child ask, 'Mummy, what are those animals doing over there?' I don't wait to hear her reply; I am too busy yelling at my daughter, 'Quickly the guinea pigs have escaped, all of them.'

And the boys, playing happily in the back garden, or so I think, before they come streaking round to the front garden and chase each other between the tables. Not only are they completely covered in mud, but they are trying to whack each other with riding crops.

As for denying my children too much sweet stuff on account of it being bad for their teeth, there's only so much room in my freezer and we are all heartily sick of leftovers.

'Oh please, do we have to eat cake again?' is their unanimous cry.

No, if I'm honest, our venture is not the resounding success we might have wished. Therefore, we decide to close after the August Bank Holiday Monday.

It is just as well. On Tuesday morning there is a knock on the door.

'Hi,' I say to a dreary little man in a tired suit. 'Can I help you?'

'Yes,' he replies. 'Is this Cottage Teas?'

'Well yes and no,' I say. 'I'm afraid if you want a cup of tea you're out of luck. I'm sure I can find you some cake. Glad to get rid of it actually.'

'I'm from Health and Safety,' he continues. 'Someone has reported you for serving food without our permission.'

'Well you're too late. We finished yesterday.'

'Just as well,' he says. 'Otherwise I would have had to fine you.'

I stand and think for a moment. 'How do I get permission if I want to cater?' I ask.

'If you give me your details, I'll send you the forms. Then it's just a matter of inspecting your premises.'

I thank him and close the door.

Chapter 33

Binding

🖋 My expensive education did not leave me hungry. With no apparent emphasis on any career, I left boarding school with a handful of O levels. Initially I wanted to go to agricultural college to study botany, but as I sat in the study being told what exams were required for acceptance I can, in all honesty, say it was the first time in my life that the penny dropped as to why exams mattered. Until then I regarded them merely as annoying little obstacles set up by some sadistic teachers to otherwise spoil the fun of school.

But this was my problem; there were many in my year who buckled down and knew where they were going.

My abiding love of books was the one constant in a life led mainly from my heart.

After my abortive attempt at finishing school and a spell in Italy, I was settled on becoming a bookbinder. It was an unusual choice, especially for a girl as it was then considered as a trade and a very male dominated one at that. One of my personal bugbears is arts and crafts, and though I like to think bookbinding falls very definitely into the latter category, I set about learning my craft at Camberwell Art School in the printing department. There was not in those days a structured syllabus for bookbinding as such; I virtually had the run of the place indulging in every avenue that took my fancy. I was in my element with handmade papers, leather and gold leaf.

However, this was in the days before student loans and it soon became apparent that I could no longer afford the luxury of art school; I needed gainful employment. With only a rudimentary knowledge of this honourable craft, I set off into the grown-up world of earning a living.

And so it was one wet, cold autumn afternoon I went about looking for my first proper job. I knew no one in the book trade so my only option was to bang on doors and sell myself. I walked up and down the wet London pavements peering through a variety of bookshop windows, while trying to galvanise the courage to present myself in a manner any potential employer might find irresistible.

Eventually, I decided to start at the top. Hatchards in Piccadilly was a fine, handsome bookshop and one I knew well. I strode in purposefully and asked an assistant where the antiquarian book department was. He directed me to the top floor. My mouth was dry and my confidence waning when an elderly man in a pinstriped suit enquired if I needed any help.

'I was wondering if you had any jobs going,' I said in a clumsy manner.

'Jobs, what kind of jobs, do you have a degree?' he replied imperiously.

'Well no, not really,' I reply, while thinking once more of my attitude towards schooling.

'No, not selling books,' I continue. 'I repair them, I'm a bookbinder.'

'Really?' he said, somewhat sceptically. 'I suppose you have your own bindery?'

'Well no, not exactly, I'm still at art school at the moment. It's just that I really need to start to work.'

He looked me up and down in a not altogether enthusiastic manner.

For my part, I was beginning to wish I had made more of an effort on the sartorial front; knee-high boots and a skirt that had once been referred to as a belt were probably not very appropriate in these hallowed environs.

'I'm afraid I can't help you,' he continued. 'We use a professional bindery for all of our binding work.' And with that he withdrew his attention and resumed his cataloguing.

'I really am sorry to bother you, but you don't happen to know anywhere else I might try?'

'There's an antiquarian bookshop in Grafton Street, at the top of Albermarle Street, but I doubt if you'll have any luck there,' he added with a tone of finality.

What light there was had already gone as I dodged my way between dripping umbrellas and puddles. I stood outside the double-fronted shop and wondered, after the last encounter, if I could possibly summon the courage to enter. The window on my left contained one book; it was published by the Trianon press and lay open to display a facsimile of a William Blake watercolour. It was exquisite. In the other window was another illustrated book, *Extinct Birds* by Lord Rothschild. Before I allowed myself to become intimidated and lose heart, I grabbed the highly polished brass handle and opened the door into another world.

How readily we jump to conclusions, make hasty assumptions, based on our own often flawed perceptions of how things appear.

I was greeted with an outstretched hand and a warm smile by a dear old-fashioned gentleman. 'You look soaked through. Can I take your coat, fetch you a cup of tea?'

'Gosh, how kind,' I said. 'No, I'm fine thanks. I just wondered if you might need a bookbinder? I'm looking for a job.'

The room was lined with glass-fronted bookcases and was heated by an old coal stove. I had walked back into the last century. Mr Dring pulled up two chairs and we sat drinking mugs of steaming hot tea. He appeared genuinely interested in my situation and sent me home with a huge leather-bound volume of *Aesop's Fables*.

'Let's see what you can do with this, it's got a broken spine,' he said, handing it to me. 'The corners could do with a bit of a repair as well.'

And with that he bade me good afternoon, with a 'Hope to see you next week,' and a smile.

The price of £245 was written in pencil inside the front cover. It was such a huge amount of money for one book that I didn't dare work on it. Instead my tutor at school repaired it. And so, on the strength of another's craftsmanship, I secured my first grown-up job as an antiquarian bookbinder.

A tiny bindery was constructed for me in the 'Occult' room on the fourth floor of this ancient building. I had to learn quickly; not only to work in vellum and reversed calf, but paper repairs and gilding. Then there were the books too precious to interfere with. For them I made boxes that resembled Morocco leather bindings; with insides lined with rich-coloured velvet. But more importantly it was here that my existing love of books took flight. Many an afternoon was whiled away reading, as opposed to repairing a book. And although my first job in the book world will always remain one of the most intensely rich seams in my life, I knew then, without a doubt, that my love of the written word far exceeded the outward appearance of a book. So when an opportunity came to move my life on in another direction, I grasped it with both hands.

✐ ✐ ✐

Chapter 34

Limbering Up

Goodness how the children grow. Only recently my first-born has ruthlessly cast aside all matters childlike and embraced the awkward phase with a vengeance.

I should have guessed by her choice of food. Tonight she insists on prawn cocktail for supper, which she eats dressed in an old ballgown and high heels, raided from the dressing-up trunk. She now aspires to an altogether different lifestyle and secretly longs to be Joan Collins in *Dynasty*. The boys and I have been banned from sitting with her as we are not taking her transition seriously enough.

But I would suggest she is not the only one who is flexing her pinions. All three appear to be mutating before my very eyes.

I have constantly urged my children to tell the truth. This is not simply for moral reasons, but also, I explain to them, because of how very complicated things can become with even the smallest untruth. They know the consequences of telling a lie.

It has occurred to me recently that I haven't seen a school

report for Dan for some time. Nowadays the children bring them home at the end of term.

'Dan, what's happened to your report?' I ask. 'I've had Joe's and Elf's – where's yours?'

He is not ruddy-cheeked like me, his skin is pale. As he looks me straight in the eye, I notice the faintest of blushes rise in his face. He shrugs his shoulders and says, 'You really wouldn't want to read them. They've not been worth reading.'

'Well, that's for me to decide. Where are they? Please go and get them.'

'I can't, I don't have them. I tore them up and chucked them out the bus window.' While I know I should be cross with him, I secretly applaud his spirit.

I am delighted to realise that my time was not completely wasted cleaning the kitchen for my cottage teas venture. I duly filled out the official forms that the man from Health and Safety sent me and executed the necessary changes that were required for me to start a catering business. I then attended a mandatory course on food hygiene and passed the exam. I have to confess the latter left me seriously wondering as to the type of person who worked in the food industry. On the very first line of the first page of the booklet they handed out, it stated, without a hint of irony, 'Always remember to wash your hands after visiting the toilet.'

And so it is I embark on yet another adventure. The local shop soon gets wind of it and before long I am baking cakes galore. The vicar's wife runs a keep-fit club and puts in a weekly order for homemade soup and rolls. Soon my arsenal extends to sandwiches, which I happily deliver within a ten-mile radius. And all by word of mouth! There is no stopping me now.

Despite my hasty departure from finishing school all those

years ago, I had still acquired a fairly good grounding in the basics. When our local museum asks if I might turn my hand to their annual dinner, my business takes flight.

Like so many things in my life, although it was not an avenue I would have taken by choice, it does, however, tick most of my requisite boxes. And as always, it results in being more than the sum of the parts.

The Elf, already showing an interest in food, is only too willing to waitress at some function or other. With Dan I am more careful; while he too is keen on earning a little extra pocket money, his leanings are more towards bar work. It is also a good excuse for Joe to increase his flock of poultry and so keep me supplied with eggs.

One novel use of his quail eggs is not only masterful, but rapidly becomes my signature dish for local drinks parties. It is fiddly in the extreme, but well worth it. Firstly you fry little rounds of bread till golden, then fry bacon till just cooked. The quail eggs are then fried till the white is firm and the yolks remain runny. Cut the bacon into pieces to fit the bread then place a fried egg on top. These are then arranged on a serving dish to await distribution.

'Dan,' I yell down the corridor. 'Dan.'

He has become more biddable with the years and only too eager to brush up on his newly acquired skill. He's just passed his driving test.

'Darling, be a love and take these up to the Pardoes. All the other bits are already in the car, but these needed to be made at the last mo,' I say, handing him the dish.

'They look good. What are they?' he says, picking one up.

'Oi! Hands off! They're tiny little fried breakfasts and they're completely irresistible. Okay, you might as well have that one, but no more.'

I hold the kitchen door open for him and help him to the car.

'What did Peter think of the quail eggs?' I ask when he gets back. 'Weren't they knocked out by them?'

He doesn't answer me, simply stands in the doorway and grins. 'I'm too old to be sent to my room now, aren't I?'

'What do you mean?'

'Well, you did say they were irresistible.'

'You little bugger. And I thought you were growing up.'

Chapter 35

Don't Believe All You Read

🖋 I'm sure I'm not the first to admit that women, or girls as we were then, of a certain age and background chose to lose their virginity on foreign shores.

I genuinely believe that getting further away from Mother and her all-seeing-ness was half of it. The other was the perceived wisdom that French, Spanish or indeed Italian *blades* were more accomplished than the spotty youths at Pony Club camp we honed our kissing skills on. Despite thinking they were pretty pathetic, I suppose they did serve their purpose.

A short walk from home across an old granite bridge was a tiny village shop. Lurking among the Rickett's blue bags, so useful for grass stains on grey ponies, paraffin oil and sherbet flying saucers, I discovered *Love Mags*. They were passports to another world. I could while away a summer's afternoon following the fate of some hapless female as she went in pursuit of love. With time-honoured formulas, it was never until the last page that our heroine found true love and always in the guise of some gorgeous-looking hunk. The narrative unfolded with pictures of the characters, little speech bubbles, some-times thought bubbles, emanating from their mouths. On the last page when *he kissed her,* stars were drawn around their heads. The artist used other symbols too, but suffice it to say, our protagonists were having a jolly time of it and normally in a swoon of sorts. This never happened in the tack room at camp.

It was Italy, Italy on a hot July night. It was dark. With Mother safely back in England and the moon shining, I could see no earthly reason not to; earthly being the operative word. Anyway there we were alfresco, and the stars shone appropriately. I lay on the bare earth and left the rest to him so to speak.

How did they *do it* in love mags? I wondered. Then suddenly I remembered that they didn't. No, the stories always ended with him clinching her in a tight embrace, her eyes invariably closed as his lips bore down on hers. Stars and exclamation marks all contrived to give a feeling of bliss, euphoria and generally being transported to hitherto unforeseen heights . . . But they didn't actually *do it.* Oh heck!

So this is it then. Here we go. Thank God it's abroad. Verbal communication was limited: my Italian was poor and his English non-existent. But there was not a lot that needed to be said.

I was completely preoccupied with thoughts of Mother when a feeling began to creep over my body bringing me sharply back into the now.

Then it started, the tingling: up my spine, down my legs and across my buttocks. The sensation became more intense and as I stared at the stars I was reminded of the last pages of the love mags.

Yes, they were right! I began wriggling . . . then prickling

. . . first my thigh and then a shoulder. Gosh, it wasn't what I had expected, but hey! Then he started . . . itching. Interesting but again not quite what I had imagined.

Gesu Cristo, he exclaimed. We were both writhing like mad now. No wonder they didn't draw this bit, I thought. His voice was rising in unison with his scratching as the whole thing become more lively and urgent. *Dio Mio.*

Gosh! I wish my Italian was better but I must be doing okay.

The feeling was becoming unbearable. I ran my hand down my legs, which were now stinging; my flesh felt as if it was alive.

Suddenly my inamorato leapt to his feet and was brushing his hands over his body, he ran about yelling loudly, *Santo cielo! Formiche rosse! Cruente formiche che mordono!* I remember the words; he repeated them so often it would have been difficult not to. I couldn't find them in my little phrase book. It was only when I could lay my hands on a proper dictionary did I discover roughly what he had said.

'Red ants! Bloody biting ants!'

🌿 🌿 🌿

Chapter 36

Winds of Change

I hate it when the swallows leave. I don't always notice the exact date but I do watch them preparing for their departure. They huddle together on the telegraph wires chattering away, making plans, then suddenly it all goes quiet.

The Elf has decided to leave school. She is not quite seventeen, and although I would rather she stayed on, she is adamant. While I am saddened by her decision, I feel it would be a little disingenuous of me to make a huge fuss given my own past history. Terry has asked her to spend the summer in Devon helping at the hotel. After this she promises to return home and go to art school in the autumn. While a part of me is heaving a huge sigh of relief as I am not finding her easy at the moment, I feel she is beginning to spread her wings. But then equally I know how close she is to my sister; they share the same artistic temperament. It will be good for her to learn to cook and a change of scenery will certainly not go amiss. I shall remain positive.

And earlier this summer Dan went to his first music concert;

I think it was Monsters of Rock at Donington. At first I was hesitant about letting him go; he seemed far too young to go anywhere without me. I still lack the confidence to make such a huge decision on my own. Fortunately the parents of the two friends he was going with were perfectly happy with the arrangements, so the choice was made for me. He returned home elated and somehow a little older. There was the distinct feeling he had shifted a little closer to the edge of the nest.

And if that isn't change enough, Maggie comes round with dramatic news. As we sit in the garden with a glass of wine surrounded by an assortment of poultry, she drops a bombshell. Well actually she doesn't, James does.

'We're moving,' he says.

'You're what?' I say, thinking I haven't heard correctly.

'I'm sorry. I didn't mean you to hear it like that. But James is right. We've decided to move. We've found a lovely old house with much more space for the children. It's near Norwich.'

All I can muster is, 'Oh no!' while tears course down my cheeks.

'Someone's already made an offer on ours so we should be gone by the end of the summer.'

My father was fond of saying, 'I don't want to know.' As a child I thought it was most odd; I wanted to know everything. I now think it very sage. Despite my constant thirst for know-ledge, there is so much in life that I would rather know nothing about . . .

I have decided to give Dan the spare bedroom. It's time the boys have a bit more space. With the Elf in Devon I shall give her room over to visitors. While my mother has constantly urged me to be more diligent in matters domestic, I always knew there was no mileage in looking under mattresses. I have resisted for long enough and now I am vindicated. As I take the double bed apart an unopened packet of condoms falls to the floor. I bend down to pick them up.

Good heavens, I think, *how on earth did those get there?*

Evidently someone has slipped them between the mattress and the base, but who, and when? I make a mental list of everyone who has slept in my rosebud-themed bedroom complete with lace curtains, and though I rack my brains I still have no idea who the culprit could be.

And if that isn't enough to put me off looking under mattresses, I then dismantle Dan's bed to take it down to his new room only to find a girlie magazine among the odd socks and mouldy pizzas. As well as, to my horror, a pile of Page Threes, taken from George's newspaper, no doubt. No wonder he kept asking what had happened to his paper.

With so very many changes going on, it's tempting to become maudlin, but I refuse to become downhearted. Instead I shall dwell on the countless happy memories that we've gathered over the years; we'll always have those.

I have a scar on my elbow. It is quite pronounced and I often find myself touching it. It serves to remind me of one of my very dearest friends. Tragically she died of cancer; it was a disfiguring facial cancer and borne so bravely. She is one of the souls I still cannot believe has gone, so I have a need to talk to her up in the ether. Her last wish was to have her ashes scattered in the outgoing tide at Walberswick by her four children and closest friends. Our plan was to scatter her ashes, then have a picnic and a game of rounders to celebrate her life and the many happy summers we had all spent together on this beach.

I parked my car and walked towards her daughter, to be greeted with, 'Oh good, here's Nicky – she'll know.'

'Know what, Jess?' I asked, leaning forward to kiss her.

'We looked up tides on the internet. Must have got it wrong. We're too early – the sea's still coming in.'

'We've decided to have the picnic and rounders first, then do the ashes later when the tide has turned,' continued one of the twins.

'I don't see a problem. So what was it you wanted to ask me?'

'It's Mum,' said Jess, lifting a maroon velvet carrier bag containing the jar of her mother's ashes from the back seat of her car. 'We don't know what to do with her. I don't like leaving her in the car alone. What do you think we should do with her?'

'I agree with you entirely. We can't possibly leave her. I vote she comes on the picnic with us.'

We had a jolly picnic with plenty of wine. And it was all the more fitting with Jan plonked in the centre of our spread. The wind blew but there she sat resolutely in the middle, lending her weight to the flimsy tablecloth.

I can't remember whose idea it was, it may well have been mine, but it seemed entirely appropriate. As we scoured the pebbly beach for suitable stumps or stops for the rounders match, we placed Jan, still draped in her elegant maroon velvet, at base.

And so not only had she participated in tea, but she was now fully engaged in our game. I was showing off as usual when I made a dash for base to enable one of the twins to get a round. I never made it; instead I slipped on a large pebble and crashed to the ground. When I stood up and pulled myself together I noticed there was blood pouring out of a deep cut on my elbow. I tied something around to staunch the flow and we continued our game until the tide turned and we could fulfil Jan's dying wish.

I now have a scar on my elbow. Often I inadvertently run my fingers over it then give a big smile. To this day I feel it is Jan continuing to make her presence felt. But more importantly it also serves to remind me, however chilling the winds of change might be, I'm still around to feel them.

Chapter 37

Pill Popping

I think I am now what is known as the 'sandwich generation'. Admittedly the Elf has all but left home with her move to Devon, but I still have Dan and Joe to look after. Now it seems that Mum may be beginning to lose some of her faculties and it will fall to me and my sister to care for her. Only recently she has been unwell; although she has made a complete recovery, it feels like an omen of what may be to come.

I have just returned from spending a few days with her and am in no doubt that while she is in very good physical shape, her mind is becoming more frail. So here I am, wedged firmly between two generations, both in need of me. And what I really want to be doing is galloping along the beach with the wind in my hair. But hey!

'Now Mum, take this pill first. You have one this morning and I'll give you the other this evening.'

'How long do I have to take these for?'

'The course is for five days. Now here, take these two, they're paracetamol.'

204

'What are they for?'

'They'll bring down your fever.'

'How do you know I've got a fever?'

'The doctor took your temperature.'

'Did she? And did I have one?'

'Yes.'

'How do you know?'

'Because I was here.'

'Were you, darling? Oh, it's awful to lose your mind. Why was the doctor here?'

'Because you went all shivery and couldn't use your legs.'

'I don't feel shivery now. I'm better, so I don't need any more pills.'

'You do,' I say very slowly and deliberately. 'It is really important that you finish the course.'

'Why?' she asks in a peevish voice.

I can't be arsed to answer. I go through to the kitchen to collect the pillbox that is delivered every Monday. It's an ingenious idea to facilitate the pill-popping that inevitably accompanies advanced years and a declining memory. There are several compartments for each day of the week. In Mother's case only one of these per day is filled, actually hardly filled. There are precisely three pills which, considering her age, don't seem very many. On the lid there is a list explaining the contents. I read this carefully and it is quite obviously vital that she takes the bright orange one daily. We have all witnessed the unedifying spectacle of her choking, when she has forgotten. The other two pills, two tiny round white ones, are nothing more than aspirin. I presume, in the absence of her doctor, that they are either a placebo or intended to assuage any residual pain from her hip operation some three years ago. As such, I make the decision to chuck them out while she is taking paracetamol.

I return to the bedroom and proffer the capsule.

'What is this for?'

'Mum, this is the pill for your oesophagus.'

'My what?'

'You know, this is the one that it is vital that you take every day.'

'Why?'

I explain.

'And how long do I have to take it for?'

'Forever.'

She places gnarled crumpled fingers to her throat and says, 'It's bloody awful getting old, you know.'

'That's as may be, but Mum, please just take this.' I hand her the capsule and a glass of water.

She swallows, and after three bodged attempts it is gone. Water drips down her chin.

'What about the little round white ones?' she asks, making me wonder just how much of her mind is actually going.

'I've thrown them away Mum.'

'Why?'

'Well, as you are taking paracetemol, I thought it best for the moment as they are similar.'

'Why am I taking paracetemol?'

I explain.

'How do you know so much about medicine?'

'I don't.'

'Well how do you know all this?'

'Because I read the packets.'

'So how long do I have to go on taking these for?'

'You take the antibiotics for another three days and the capsule for the rest of your life.'

'Why do I need antibiotics?'

'Because you have a kidney infection.'

'Have I? I wonder how I got a kidney infection.' She addresses the ceiling.

'I suspect it has something to do with the amount of alcohol you consume at the expense of water or other liquids,' I quip unnecessarily.

'But I haven't had a drink for three days,' she says, not only with vehemence, but also accuracy.

Again I mentally question the efficacy of her, self-confessed, dwindling powers of recollection. At times it appears to my sister and me that it veers a tad on the side of selective.

'You don't think I could have a little drink now do you?'

'No.'

'Well I'm jolly well going to have a fag!'

I sit watching this extraordinary spectacle. Six attempts at lighting up. Her poor arthritic hands grasp the matches in an awkward, clumsy manner and each broken unignited match is tossed in the air with an almost childlike petulance. The floor is littered. The occasional match bursts into flame on its descent. It is quite alarming, not to mention a little dangerous. I am mesmerised. This is the same woman who once berated me for smoking; was once so incredibly fastidious, so house-proud.

'Oh do have a fag, darling. They don't do you any harm.'

I vacillate between feeling hugely protective, exasperated, mildly irritated, then ultimately such pathos.

Where will it end? In a puff of the proverbial smoke, if she goes on like this.

Chapter 38

A Bad Habit

I suppose it is inevitable, given one is blessed with family, that at some point roles will begin to reverse. I am convinced I started smoking as an act of rebellion against my parents. That and a pathetically naive assumption that it made me look cool. While I do not think for a moment the latter is a contributing factor to my mother having taken up the habit, I am in no doubt there is a touch of the insurgence in her action.

I've smoked for the best part of forty years, and for over half of those I have longed to give up. It began at school; prefects would give us cigarettes in exchange for running errands. I remember coughing violently and thinking how disgusting they where but I persevered. I was diligent in my application to acquire the habit. They were the passport to evolution.

On my sixteenth birthday I lit up in front of my horrified parents, but they were no longer in a position to stop me. Since then I must have tried to give up twenty times.

I have tried replacement therapy and endless expensive patches. But my mind is devious and at times leads a life of its own. I went to a family wedding in the West Indies. It was very hot, I sweated and we swam a lot. The patches floated away along with my good intentions. So you see it wasn't my fault. It was the heat.

Then I tried hypnosis. The idea was that you do not give up immediately but gradually begin to cut down. It worked up to a point, but then I fell off my horse and hurt my collar bone. I needed to compose myself and for a smoker there is only one way: with what I knew best.

I met an old acquaintance, someone I remember as having chain-smoked and who I had never credited with being overly intelligent. When I asked her if she still smoked, her reply was a resounding, 'No! I want to be around to see my grandchildren grow up . . .'

It's becoming ever more difficult to smoke in public. There are increasingly fewer homes of friends where you dare to ask if they 'mind'. The most salient point I remember is how easy it is to squander time, in the cinema, at the theatre, on trains, always wishing time away so that you can light up.

I have always rolled my own cigarettes so cost is not the issue. But the constant nagging worry of running out of papers, tobacco or matches, especially on a Sunday night, bordered on the possessed. In the depths of the country, driving miles to avoid such a panic, began to occur to me as utterly futile. Not for the first time I was beginning to annoy myself.

There is definitely a burgeoning feeling of the tail wagging the dog.

The final kick up the proverbial for me was when I sat in a hospice watching my dear friend Jan slip away. She died from a very invasive, disfiguring cancer. The surgeon was big enough to say, 'I have no idea', when I ask him if smoking had been a contributory factor in her death. A profound factor, for me, however, is the presence of her four marvellous children. Each one has put their young lives on hold, be it backpacking, touring with a pop group or finishing a much-coveted degree. They are selfless in their daily vigil at their mother's bedside. It is then that I make my resolve. We none of us can know the manner of our going. But sure as anything, if one persists in smoking the chances of having a lingering, painful, undignified end is more likely. If there is a way I can avoid inconveniencing my family, quitting smoking must be high on the list.

The National Health Service runs a series of ads urging smokers to phone a helpline or contact their GP, who invariably refer you to a clinic to help the would-be 'giver upper'. I phone the former. Having answered a legion of questions, the anonymous voice says something along the lines of really why was I even bothering, given my advanced years.

'That does it!'

I make an appointment to see a nurse at my local surgery. She is charming, explains all the options to me, but more importantly, she is completely unjudgemental. My choice is a drug called Zyban. It works thus: for the first week you keep smoking while taking one tablet a day. On the seventh day you take two tablets and give up smoking on the eighth. Well, in theory you do.

As I said, the mind has a mind of its own. My seventh day falls on a Sunday. It also happens to be the day I am driving to Devon to see Mum. Three hundred boring miles, alleviated only by chain-smoking. My packing is such that the tablets get mislaid in the chaos. So not only do I not take the first, but I also miss taking the second. Great! I think. I can't possibly give up tomorrow. Excellent! So I smoke all evening.

The next morning I put the kettle on and start to roll a cigarette when the freakiest thing happens. It is as if someone is sitting on my shoulder.

'Who are you kidding?' it says to me. 'Are you really serious about giving up or not? The only person you're letting down is yourself.'

I physically turn and listen to this inner dialogue. Then I walk over to the bin and trash everything: tobacco, papers, the lot.

And that was it. I have not touched a cigarette since. And I know I'll never smoke again. Quitting has empowered me in a way that nothing else has ever done. I have an abiding feeling of 'if I can crack smoking, then I can crack anything'.

Chapter 39

Blind Date

With the all the children in Devon for the summer holidays, I swing between enjoyment of my new-found freedom and a sense of foreboding; I am aware I have become more of a recluse. An old friend of mine has been urging me to meet a friend of his. I think he said something along the lines of a blind date. It's a dreadful expression and makes me cringe. He himself has a new girlfriend and suggested that we all meet up for dinner, but I have an overriding fear that I am being set up.

I sit in the back of the taxi wondering whatever possessed me to get talked into this. As I prepared to go out, I tried to think of a valid excuse for cancelling the whole silly idea. But I couldn't. I am not given to swanning about in taxis, but frankly I am so anxious I fear drink might be taken.

'Where did you say you wanted to get dropped off?' says the driver.

I had agreed to meet them all in the restaurant but my nerves are getting the better of me and it still isn't too late to do a runner.

'If you drop me in Castle Street, that would be just fine,' I say, feeling that to walk the last hundred yards will give me time to either compose myself or bolt.

'And what time do you want picking up?' he asks.

Goodness, what have I let myself in for? Peter, our mutual friend, the one I have to thank, or blame, for getting me into this dilemma, insisted that Jack and I would hit it off immediately. For my part I am yet to be convinced.

I find myself dithering. 'I'm not really sure, I may just be getting a lift home.'

'Tell you what. If I don't hear from you by ten-thirty, I'll assume you're sorted. How does that suit you?' he says.

What a nice man, I think as I pay him. 'Thank you so much,' I say, 'I may just see you later.'

He gives me a big wink, and says, 'Best of luck!'

As I falter at the door, the first person I see is Peter. He walks towards me grinning from ear to ear.

'Well done,' he says, 'I honestly thought you wouldn't come.'

'This is Jane,' he continues, leading me up to the table. But I am not looking at her. There, standing beside my chair is the gorgeous-looking man who had caught my eye in the pub all those years ago.

For the life of me I cannot remember my reply. I am too busy staring into a pair of blue eyes.

✍ I remember the phone call as if it were yesterday. It was just after Mum's very first visit to the cottage.

'Oh darling, I do wish there was more I could do to help,' she said, sounding genuinely concerned.

'Please don't worry,' I said. 'I'm okay. Actually I've met this really nice chap and it's all going fine.'

'How lovely darling, I'm so pleased,' she continued. After the exchange of further niceties we hung up.

Within minutes the phone rang again. It was Mum playing a different fiddle. 'Did I hear correctly?' she barked. 'You mean you've met another man?'

'Yes, Mum, but it's early days. I'm not sure what will happen.'

'I know exactly what will happen, young lady. Two wrongs don't make a right. You nip this one in the bud, right now.'

'But Mum, he makes me happy.'

'That's not the point,' she continued. 'What your children need now is you – one hundred per cent of you. They asked for none of this. If you start dividing your attention you will regret it. Mark my words.' Then the line went dead.

For someone who's spent the greater part of her life not listening to her mother, this advice resonated. I looked about me and saw a grain of truth.

I finished the relationship, there and then. And it was many years before I felt ready to embark on another.

⁂

Oddly enough I didn't resent these pearls of wisdom. Far from it, it was very sound council. Since then, I've thrown myself into being a full-time mother unfettered by the distractions of another liaison, just as she suggested. The children have all been terrific and they've had my undivided attention, but now I realise they not only don't need it, they no longer want it. They are beginning to follow their own stars. Perhaps I should too.

It is heaven on that first morning, turning over in bed and finding that after all these years, I am not alone. As I lie there going through every detail of the previous evening I glance at the clock, leap out of bed and start to pull on some clothes.

'Whatever are you doing?' enquires a sleepy voice. 'Come back to bed.'

'I'd love to,' I say, 'but there's no time.'

'What do you mean? It's not even seven yet.'

'I know,' I say, 'but I have to collect the papers and deliver them. Dan's away in Devon.'

There is a long silence. Then a pondering, 'That's the first time I've ever slept with a paper boy,' emanates from my bed.

Now that Jack is in my life, I think his most sterling quality is his lack of self. Never once has he ever imposed his views on me or the children. There is a gentle acceptance that it is my role to be a mother, and his not to interfere.

Other than in matters practical.

Rose is about to make her now annual appearance at the Palm Sunday service, but her hooves are too long. To my shame, I only notice the day before when there is little hope of getting a farrier. I mention this to Jack.

'I'll trim her feet,' he says immediately.

'What do you mean, you'll do them?'

'I was apprenticed to a farrier when I was a lad. I'll do it.'

And he does.

He constantly gives at a time when many take.

And of course he is fiendishly good-looking. I am ever so slightly alarmed that this should be one of the criteria, having berated my mother over the years for judging people thus. He sits well on a horse and after the initial attraction I suppose it was matters equine that sealed it. Sprat calls him Old Chatterbox. It's true he's a man of few words. It hadn't struck me before she said it, but I now realise it's part of his charm. Not only does his silence give us more 'airtime', but he is endearingly hesitant about boring us with his opinions.

I love the way he knocks on the door. Even after we get to know each other much better, he never presumes to walk straight in unlike everyone else. He exudes a respect for my space, both mentally and physically.

And when I do call 'Come in,' he's there with his handsome, freshly scrubbed face; a bottle in one hand and flowers or a pheasant in the other.

'I've brought you a load of wood,' is my favourite. He is generous to a fault.

I find meanness one of the most offputting of attributes. In my experience I would almost go so far as to say that those who display a mean streak with matters monetary equally manifest a meanness of spirit.

When my first love asked me to marry him I said, 'Yes,' and put on his ring.

He said 'Good, now we can sleep together.'

I remember thinking, 'Oh no, we can't,' and said as much.

He became petulant. 'But I've bought a packet of . . . I can't waste them. What am I supposed to do with them now?'

I told him, and then left.

The next morning I threw his ring into the river.

But the seal of approval, no higher praise, comes from my dear neighbour Emmi.

She stopped me the other day. And with a twinkle in her eye, she said, 'You think yourself lucky, girl. If I were forty years younger – you'd have to watch out.'

And Jack thinks the world of her, too.

Chapter 40

Easter

Of all our festivals Easter is my favourite, without a doubt. There is an urgency about Christmas with all its rituals that can so readily rob us of the true meaning.

This year Good Friday is the most beautiful calm day. It has an intangible feeling that so often eludes me at Christmas; and here it is all around. Easter stands for new beginnings and it feels very right to approach such a festival in such a way.

I pull up in my drive behind Sprat's car; she is earlier than I expected. The boys and I fall out of the car in our rush to be the first to greet her. I'd left the back door open in case we weren't home, but as I shout along the corridor there is no reply.

'She's here,' yells Dan. 'She's down the garden, collecting eggs . . . as usual.'

Oh goodness, I thought, *I know exactly what she'll do, she's such a townie.*

I scream as I run towards the hen run, 'Don't touch the clutch of eggs under Mrs Frizzle. She's sitting and they're about to hatch.'

I'm too late.

'Look,' she says. 'look how may eggs I found in one nest.'

I could hit her. 'You idiot,' I say. 'You idiot, she's been sitting on those for nearly three weeks and they were going to hatch on Easter morning. 'You've well and truly buggered them up.'

Over the years we've developed our very own little customs. And Sprat has just scuppered my favourite: to have a clutch of newly hatched chicks on Easter morning.

'I'm so sorry, Nick. I completely forgot,' she says, putting on the kettle.

Joe is laughing, 'Don't worry,' he says. 'I think we're getting a bit old for all of this anyway.'

'Oh darling, please,' I say, trying to cuddle him. 'You can never be too old for chicks. You used to love it.'

He pulls away with an embarrassed shrug of his teenage shoulders.

'Come on, let's take our tea outside. I've got lots to tell you before the others arrive,' I say to Sprat.

The back garden is always at its best in the spring. We sit under the apple tree and watch as a hen struts past, clucking away to her brood.

'Goodness, Joe's growing up,' says Sprat.

'Don't I know it, he's lost complete interest in all this lot,' I say, waving my hand around our assortment of poultry.

'So what's new, who else is coming for Easter?'

'Guess what?', I say, 'the Elf's coming back.'

'What? For good? I thought she'd settled in Devon,' says Sprat.

'Well she has, more or less. As you know I really wanted her to come back and go to art school but she seems to love it down there. And at least there's Terry and Mum to keep an eye on her. But I've got a feeling there may be a little bit more to it.'

As I speak the words I can hear a car pull up in the drive. 'Quick,' I say, 'I think it's them.'

'What do you mean, *them*?' says Sprat.

We run round to the front garden in time to greet my first-born as she walks across the lawn. Beside her is a tall, handsome youth in his early twenties.

I fling my arms around her and she hugs me back.

'Nick,' she says, pulling away from me, 'this is Luke.'

Another of our Easter rituals is copious amounts of lemon curd for the breakfast table. I say copious, that is if Sprat hasn't eaten the lot first. The only other person I can remember being so gluttonous over it was my father.

'I think you've just met a very good reason for the change of plan,' says Sprat, spooning in another mouthful.

'You may well be right,' I say. 'Do you have to eat it all? It makes me feel quite sick watching you.'

The Elf appears in the kitchen doorway and gives me one of her big open smiles. To my delight I notice she is growing her hair once more. 'Luke and I were wondering if you needed a hand?' she asks.

'Oh my darling, it is so good to have you back,' I say, throwing my arms around her again. 'I tell you what, I think this calls for a celebration. Why don't you get a bottle from the pantry and pour us all a drink?'

Easter breakfast is later than it used to be; it is also more restrained. Gone are the squeals of excitement as a newly hatched duckling peeps out of a cardboard egg or the thrills of the Easter egg hunt for the umpteenth time.

'Do you have anything for a headache?' says Dan, who is the last to put in an appearance.

'Go and look in the optimistic medicine cabinet,' says Sprat, finishing off the lemon curd.

'Whatever do you mean by optimistic?' I ask.

'Well there's nothing nasty in it. It's all aftersun or cream for insect bites. And perhaps a little something for a hangover,' she says, smiling at Dan.

'Now who's ready for the Easter egg hunt?' I volunteer as I begin to clear the table.

'Oh please Nick, do us a favour,' said Joe.

'Well you can count me out. I'm going back to bed, my head is really thumping,' says Dan, who has been uncharacteristically quiet over breakfast.

'Come on you two,' says Sprat, putting an arm around our little lovebirds. 'Elfie, you used to love egg hunts. Don't you remember we had to keep hiding them over and over again when you were all little?'

Luke stands up and begins to help me with the plates. 'Why don't I wash up while you go and play?'

For old times' sake, Sprat and I skip about the garden hiding eggs in all the most unlikely places. But really, we needn't bother.

'Where's Doris these days?' asks the Elf. 'I'd love to go and see her.'

'Well,' I say, 'I was going to mention it to you. I've put her in foal.'

Before I have time to add, 'and Jack's taken her back to the farm', I think I see a fleeting glance in Luke's direction.

'Sid has Rose at the monastery. She's so happy there,' I continue.

As I speak we hear the unmistakable sound of horse's hooves on the road.

'Quick,' I say. 'Run out, it's Sid, I'm sure he'd love to take you for a drive!'

There is only room for two passengers in the little cart, so Luke and Elfie climb in. As Sixpence trots away towards the forest, we watch them as they huddle together. And I remember something my mother-in-law was fond of saying: 'Enjoy the children while they are young. They're not yours, you know. They're only lent to us for a while.'

Sprat turns to me and voices my thoughts. 'They look pretty serious about each other. What do you think?'

'I think you may well be right,' I say again. 'Now come on, who's for church?'

In all honesty, I was so involved in my roles of mother and daughter that the dubious pleasures of becoming a grand-mother had never entered my head.

So I admit when the idea was first mooted, it did come as a bit of a shock. But that was only momentarily. I now see all the advantages.

'You're far too young to be a granny,' does wonders for my ego. I love it.

On a practical level, the row of Wellington boots in the corridor, all the tiny little ones I could never bring myself to get rid of, they're all back in use. And instead of having to relegate the Lego to the attic, I simply send it south.

Part Three

Autumn

Chapter 41

A Celebration

I love coming to stay at the farm. There is a timeless quality about the place. The first time Jack brought me here I thought I was stepping back into another century.

I have done my fair share of moving house – not always by choice. Jack, I find, not only lives in the house he grew up in, but actually sleeps in the room in which he was born. There is a permanence to his life that has continually eluded me. Yet I yearn for it.

Knowing how much I adore flowers, Jack has filled the bedroom with my favourites. I awake in the night and listen for the familiar sound of the sea crashing onto the shingle, but there is a silence and the air is thick with the heady scent of lilies. Outside in the rookery, the drawn-out hooting of a tawny owl reminds me where I am; not on the very brink of the seashore but in the heart of the countryside. And it feels so very right. I feel a renewed optimism about the future.

I have at last acquired a good habit; oddly enough from my sister. Every morning I go for a bracing walk – it sets me up for the day. Dogs are one of the few animals we have never had at the cottage. I have always felt they are too needy and would be too much of an extra burden. When I spend time at the farm Jack has dogs enough for us both.

For so long I have taken too much for granted; always accepting my good health and fortune, sometimes in a curmudgeonly way and at others, less than graciously. Not now. I am genuinely happy to greet each day anew, with its sights, smells, sounds, but for how long, who knows?

The puppies' enthusiasm knows no bounds. Despite missing out on a walk the previous evening, they hold no grudges. They do not berate or judge me, but simply grasp the moment: this moment. A joyous early autumn moment and their ebullience is contagious.

The change in the air is palpable, but only just. I try to quantify just why September feels so very different, but no such ruminations for Millie and Pip. For them it is quite simply the joy of being alive, rushing about putting up a hare in the fresh plough. Or leaping into the air in a vain attempt to pluck a skylark as she is shocked out of the stubble. Watching them lifts my spirit and is joy enough.

Never have I seen the hedgerows so full of fruits and berries; a wealth of rich edible jewels. I feast my eyes on the colours: there is all the richness of Caravaggio's palette. Deep red haws with the greenest of foliage. The blues of the sloes still cowled in their unearthly grey pallor. The almost black elderberries bleeding magenta juices down their stalks where the birds have feasted, all framed with shades of gold of the now turning field maple.

It is as if some unseen force is draining the colour not just from a wayfarer bush here or a guelder rose there, but from the very days themselves. I feel a deep pathos on such a morning and the beauty of it stills me. Yes, we have all grumbled about the lost summer; the wet, the cold, the incessant grey days. But despite nature's inclemency, she still showers us with her bounty.

There is a richness and substance to this season like no other. Winter is all thinness, spring has her frailties, and as for summer, she is so full of promise she is destined to disappoint. Could it be we have no expectation of autumn and as such, she never fails to please?

A silver sun rises above the skyline into a colourless day. Last night's hunter's moon tarries on the horizon and for a moment I cannot distinguish one from the other. The light has defined the monotones of the distant hedgerows and trees in a way that were I an artist, I would at last be able to understand perspective. A faraway mist lends an eeriness to the silence. Cobwebs, bright with dew drops, span twigs and grasses. There is such a stillness in the grey expressionless sky. It reminds me of the oddest question Dan ever asked me. It was on such a washed out sort of a day he inquired wistfully – all seven years of him – if the world was only black and white when I was young. And this morning it feels that perhaps it was.

The leaves are just beginning to turn. The last few days have been warm, sunny and completely wonderful. I have not made, nor have any desire to make, jellies or jams. However, a part of me looks at the berries and feels it is almost sinful to pass them by. In truth though, the cupboard is full of last year's jars, not to mention the sloe gin. Things were so very different when the children were young. With only Joe left at home now, and even he seems to spend more and more time with his friends, there's only Jack and me to feed. And with the continual thickening of the girth, the less I mess about with matters culinary the better.

Chapter 42

A Family Christmas

Such is my dear sister's passion for gold and glitter, coupled with an unquenchable desire for fairy lights, that in her house it is hard to determine when it actually is Christmas. John, her long-suffering husband, displays a tolerance of her questionable taste that some among us feel borders on the saintly.

But her house will make the most perfect venue for a huge combined family Christmas. Given Mother's advanced years, we've made the unanimous decision to get everyone together. It may well be our last opportunity.

We make a list of all the players. There is of course Mum. Then Terry, John and their three boys, then there is me and my lot. Elfie and Luke now have three young children – Billie, Tobi and Felix – and live only miles away from Terry. Dan is now living in Bristol, so he's joining us with his girlfriend and lastly, of course, Joe. Sadly Jack can't make it.

'What time does the plane get in?' I ask my sister.

'What plane? Get in where?' says Mum.

'Mum, we've told you a hundred times. Mark and Shareen are coming over for Christmas.'

'What do you mean? Coming over from where?' she asks.

'The West Indies,' says Terry, flashing me an exasperated look.

'Whatever are they doing there?' says Mum.

'That's where they live.'

'Nice tree,' I say to my sister, changing the subject.

'I can't be bothered with a tree this year,' says Mum.

'You won't have to bother. We're doing it,' I say. Then, to my sister, 'Well done for getting one that's still growing – we can plant it in the garden afterwards.'

'After what?' asks Mum.

'Christmas,' I shout. 'Look, I'll leave you and Terry to dress it. I must go and finish wrapping prezzies.'

'I think Christmas is overrated. It's a complete bore. Why do you have to make such a fuss? I don't want a tree. What do I want with one at my age?'

'Well, we thought it would be nice if everyone came here after church. You know, for a little drink before we have lunch with Terry and John.'

'Who's everyone?'

'Mum, for the umpteenth time, we're all going to be together for Christmas; all of us. It'll be wonderful,' I say. I run through the list once more as her face becomes glummer and glummer.

As if by magic, we awake to a winter wonderland. It's the first white Christmas for some of the little ones and simply adds to the excitement of what we hope will be the perfect Christmas.

After church we drive back down into the valley as large flakes of snow float through the air. The children peer out of the car windows and beam.

Mum's little cottage looks so inviting under its fringe of thatch. Inside, we have put on a CD of carols and I know we did the right thing by insisting on decorating a tree.

She sits by a roaring fire and I watch as her great-grandchildren mill around proffering drinks and eats.

'Would any of you like a cigarette?' she asks, opening a box and waving it under my young granddaughter's nose.

We all look on in horror.

'Mum, shut up, they're far too young. Anyway you're the only one that smokes nowadays and I'd rather you didn't light up in front of them.'

There follows a petulant silence, before Mum asks, 'Are any of you youngsters married?'

'Mum, please.'

'Please what? It's a perfectly normal question.'

'Look, it's Christmas day. Let's leave it,' I say, nudging her discreetly.

'Why are you kicking me, have I said something?'

'Look, it's not important. Leave it.'

'So it's alright for this lot to live together and have babies, but I'm not allowed to smoke. I think the world's gone barmy.'

'And do you know,' she continued, 'I'm jolly glad I'm old. I couldn't cope with modern living.'

After lunch we send all the little ones into the television room, while John goes off to change. We have planned for him to walk down the steps to the house jingling some bells, then knock loudly on the door.

Terry and I will then send one of the children to open it. All the while going, 'Hark! Whatever do you think that noise could be? Listen, listen, do you think it might be Santa?'

Well, that is the plan.

John walks through the kitchen complete with red coat and

trousers. He has donned a white cotton wool beard and stuck a pixie hat on his head. To add to the charade he has, rather unnecessarily in my opinion, stuffed a cushion up his front and, I have to admit, looks completely stupid.

But hey! The grandchildren are still young; they won't take much convincing.

We watch John go out into the snow-covered garden, then wait until we hear the first jingle of bells.

'Quick!' we shout to the children. 'Quick, there's someone coming!'

The children rush into the huge hallway and push their faces up against the frosted windows.

'Who do you think it could be?' I ask, as I pick up Felix and try to make him look in the direction of the bells.

'Look, here he comes, I can see him. I think it might be Father Christmas,' says my sister. 'I wonder what he might have in his sack for you.'

The children clap their hands with excitement.

'It's John in a ridiculous costume,' says Mum.

I shoot her a withering look.

But it is a memorable day; for Mum to be surrounded by her two daughters, six grandchildren, seven great-grandchildren and with an assortment of spouses and partners, all actively enjoying each other's company. It is a massive testament to her abiding spirit.

Chapter 43

Let Them Eat Cake

Dividing Christmas between my daughter and my sister has necessitated using the car boot as a repository for all things festive.

On Christmas morning, round a big roaring fire, I joined my grandchildren in all the chaos and magic of the day. I watched as the older two delighted in the gaily foil-wrapped chocolate Santas I had given them. I even smiled indulgently when the oldest accused the youngest of having chewed his.

'Oh Felix, Felix you've chewed mine.'

'Yeah, he's chewed mine too,' said the other.

On closer inspection the chocolate figures did show signs of being nibbled, but nothing too serious. Given his tender age, his lack of mobility, and only the odd cursory tooth, it was highly unlikely that Felix was the culprit. Scooping up all the chocolates I resolved to take them back to the shop and give the manager a bollocking.

After Christmas, I waltz into the shop armed with chewed Santas and demand an explanation, mindful that I am actually more annoyed with myself for not noticing the imperfections in the first place. But then, at this time of the year everything is slightly manic. The manager is charm personified. He is not aware of this ever happening before and leads me to a box of unsold Santas, now reduced in price. Here we proceed to inspect each and every one. Try as we might, we fail to find any in a similar condition to mine.

'I'm sorry Madam, but as you can see, these ones are completely untouched. We will of course replace yours, but it does look suspiciously like a mouse to me.' A mouse indeed! I feign shock horror and leave.

As I recount the conversation later, memories of a nibbled banana flash across my mind. Slowly it dawns on me that the mouse must somehow be living in my car. Have you ever heard anyone say, 'There is never just one mouse'? Please, dear reader, believe it.

I purchase and set two mouse traps, of the spring-set variety, in my car. I jest not: I catch nine mice in rapid succession. Not a particularly edifying experience as they are, on closer inspection, dear little creatures. I resolve after this mass slaughter to buy a humane mouse trap. They work on the same principle as a lobster pot and are very effective.

After a massive family Christmas in Devon, I head back to my beloved Suffolk. With the kitchen at the farm being overly warm and brimming with dogs, what remains of the Christmas cake is perched on top of an old microwave in the pantry. Imagine my surprise when I recognise the teeth marks through the icing and into the marzipan. I position the lobster pot where the cake had been, bait it with said cake, and lo and behold, in the morning there indeed is the dearest little doe-eyed mouse.

And herein lies the problem. Endless children's books

eulogise these tiny mammals. Dressed in frocks, they scuttle about in Beatrix Potter's dolls house; in Bramley Hedge they live the country idyll. In *Wind in the Willows* we even find them carol singing, no less. It has bothered me for years that Virginia Woolf spent pages describing the death of a moth in her eponymous essay. Why did she not just open the window? Instead she wrote copious prose as she watched it beating itself to death before her eyes. Great writer she may be, but reading that quite put me off her.

I digress.

7:30 am, muffled to the top of my head, finds me trudging up the field with the dogs; stick in one hand and humane mouse trap complete with small rodent in the other. The puppies are fascinated and keep jumping up. The wind blows dreadfully and it feels very cold. I peer into the trap. Two large soft brown eyes engage mine, and now I know why executioners, or perhaps it's the one to be executed, wear a hood. My resolve is blown. It's far too cold out here to let it go. Is it a town mouse or a country mouse? What on earth will it find to eat when it's used to Christmas cake? Where will it sleep? Perhaps it's got a family, babies even, back in the pantry, all waiting for it. No, this I cannot do! It's one thing for it to die quickly in a trap, but this is simply a slow torture. He is the very epitome of the famous 'wee sleekit cowrin' timorous beastie' ...

Good old Robbie Burns to the rescue. That's it! The mouse comes home. Back in the pantry I open the cage and it scuttles off; the cake I tuck on the floor behind the fridge.

'Did you catch the mouse?' asks Jack, over breakfast.

'I did,' I reply.

'Good. You know there is never just one mouse.'

Chapter 44

Empty Nest Syndrome

This fact fascinates me, I ponder on it endlessly: *The closer an animal has been to man*, in evolutionary terms that is, *the shorter the name, i.e. cow, dog, nag, pig and so on*. Actually, it makes sense when you think about it. I mean you would hardly say I must go and milk the Tyrannosaurus Rex, now would you?

Jack keeps two pigs at the farm, both sows. One is a Large Black called Sprat, after my old friend. When he tells me what he is to name her I am slightly taken aback.

'Don't you think she might be a tad insulted?' I wonder.

'It's not meant as an insult,' he replies 'I just thought they've both got such healthy appetites.'

The other is an Essex Saddleback named Darcey, Darcey Bussell really, after the principal ballerina at the Royal Ballet. Pigs have the most extraordinarily dainty feet.

Nevertheless, having these two does not merit keeping a boar. I once did a 'Pig-Keeping' course many years ago. Contrary to visions of a pig and its issue gambolling in an orchard, the reality turned out to be altogether different. Firstly, it was intensive pig-keeping. I was the only girl among some fairly fruity lads and along with the best of them I learnt to castrate piglets. The tiny testes were thrown unceremoniously into the straw where the others rooted around and ate them. At that point, I excused myself, retired to another sty and threw up. Lest I appeared girly, I said nothing.

For ages, I put this down to my delicate disposition. Then I discovered I was pregnant.

Another social asset acquired on the course was learning to artificially inseminate a sow. We watched an elementary film on the subject, made in a homespun way by the Ministry of Agriculture. They urged the utmost hygiene while carrying out this precise procedure. To that end they showed an Aga in a farmhouse with several pans on the hob all bubbling away; peas in one, potatoes in another, and all manner of rubber tubes and instruments required for artificially inseminating, in another.

Recently, Jack decided to resort to this method. He heard about the service from a member of the local smallholder's society. 'Nothing to it,' I believe were her words.

The first I knew of it was when he asked me if I had any KY jelly. Bit of a conversation stopper really, but hey . . . I'm fairly broad-minded. The semen it seems, or should I be more specific, the plastic bottles containing such, must not be shaken, but it is suggested that they should be placed in your pocket to warm before use. The instructions that come with all the necessary equipment, eye-watering to behold, are graphic in the extreme. And while I shan't expand on them any further, the last line is a winner: 'If the semen is flowing onto your boots the sow is not going to get pregnant.'

Perhaps after all it's easier to resort to the more traditional method. When Jack collected the sows from the boar, we believed Sprat would 'pig' first, Darcey at least a month later. Sprat showed absolutely no signs whatsoever, but when I suggested that Darcey had changed shape and perhaps might farrow sooner, it fell upon deaf ears. The next morning we find her surrounded by fourteen piglets; a huge first litter and only one dead.

Saddlebacks have a pink band over their shoulders so all the babies look as if they are wearing T-shirts. They are adorable and much time is wasted simply standing and staring. Mum is huge and the babes tiny, but she is completely enchanting with them. They, in turn, rather love her, and quite rightly. Every so often one will leave off from feeding and wander round to her not insubstantial mouth and give her a little kiss, or so it seems. It is captivating.

Darcey proves the most wonderful of mothers; from being a gentle, affable sort of a sow, with motherhood comes a terrifying aggression. Quite literally, I think, she would try to kill anyone who comes between her and her litter. Only a skilled pig man would suffice to cut their teeth and give them their iron injections. Interestingly it is no longer deemed necessary to de-ball the boys.

Traditionally, piglets are weaned at around six weeks, but thirteen youngsters is a lot. Darcey, despite being fed whatever she can clear up, shows signs of 'going behind' as they say. Her backbone and ribs begin to protrude in a horrific way. We decide to take the piglets away from her and wean them early. They are, after all, capable of eating creep feed. So, on a bright sunny morning we gently drive the little family out to the meadow, the idea being that mum will draw the babies into an arc at night, and when they have grasped this we will take her away. On the third day, we lead Darcey back to the freshly littered yard for a bit of hard-earned peace and quiet.

What happens next is concerning. She throws herself down in the straw and lies there refusing both food and drink. No amount of prodding or cajoling can shift her. We tempt her with all manner of delicacies, to no avail. She has completely given up.

Eventually we call the vet. He suggests a virus and administers a massive injection. I remain unconvinced. 'Within twenty-four hours the medicine will kick in, she will be back on her feet and eating,' he says. 'If not, it is more serious and as such incurable. Ring me tomorrow.'

The next day she still has not budged. I ring the vet. He suggests he should come and 'euthanise' her. His word. We decline.

Back in the yard I sit down in the straw, my hand stroking the dear face. Her eyes have a wistful, faraway look.

'Jack, I am convinced she's pining,' I say.

Vets don't think like that; nor indeed do most farmers.

I scratch her between the ears and urge her to eat the piece of apple I have bitten off for her. This she rolls around in her mouth in a cursory fashion. I force water down with the aid of a watering can. She registers her disgust by trying to turn her head away and pathetically thrashing the air with her forelegs. It is pitiful to watch. She becomes weaker by the day.

'Jack, please can we give her a couple of her babies back? I'm sure she's missing them.'

'Don't be daft. Animals don't have those sorts of feelings. Anyway, what if she's got a disease, what then? She'll end up giving it to two perfectly healthy weaners.'

To be honest, I hadn't thought of that.

The next day I repeat my little ritual: water from the watering can, apples, and lots of scratching behind her big soft ears. Her legs now are too weak to flail; all she manages is a doleful sigh. I can hardly bear it.

With tears coursing down my cheeks I jump up and scream, 'Bloody well get a grip! Eat damn you!' Uncontrollably, I throw apples all around her and run back to the house.

'Jack, please, I beg of you : . . she'll be dead by tomorrow. Please let's risk it and give her babies back,' I plead.

Whether for me, for Darcey, or quite simply to keep the peace, I shall never know. All I remember is looking up from where I am keeping vigil to see Jack with a squealing piglet under each arm.

'There you go. Try it if you must, but it won't make a ha' penny's worth of difference. And believe me, whatever she's got, they'll get.'

So withdrawn is the old girl I don't think she even registers her babies. They in turn, with only one thing on their mind, go straight to her bag, which they pummel away at with their snouts; all to no avail as she has dried up.

'There you go. You see, they'll just be a bloody nuisance. Just like I said. I don't know why I ever listen to you.'

'Please, please just let's see.'

Realising there is nothing to be had, the piglets soon leave off from their suckling and begin to root around for any discarded apples or tempting bits that are lying about. There are squeals and snufflings, but most importantly, they cuddle up to her.

I wish I could say that by the next day all is well. It isn't, but I swear that Darcey regains her will to live.

It is a long old haul. She doesn't have strength enough in her back legs to stand up for some months. We fear she might never walk again. Gradually though, with access to her

Chapter 45

God's a Bugger

Having the lunch party outside was my idea. I would lie if I said it was purely for aesthetic reasons. Quite frankly the smell in Mum's house is nothing to celebrate. Rather than embarrass my elderly mother, we tend to blame the dog, a diminutive, equally ancient, terrier. Whenever we mention it, however discreetly, the reply is always, 'It's Clarissa, poor thing. She's getting too fat to fit through the cat flap.'

But hey! The sun shines, lending the garden an appropriate air of occasion.

Given how confused dear Mum gets these days, I felt it safer to invite only a few. Felix, my youngest grandson, was dumped on me at the last minute.

I phone my cousin Anna to ask her and her mother, Aunty Dot. I also include Aubrey, our vicar, who happens to live next door to Anna. Unfortunately, as she is working, it falls to my lot to collect Aunty Dot.

'Do cover the seats with something,' Anna warns. 'Sound the horn when you arrive, otherwise she probably won't hear you. Check the key's in her bag, not behind the door. Oh, and lastly do make sure she's remembered to put her pads on.'

There are some things in life you just don't want to know about.

I lead Mum gingerly into the garden and settle her under the shade of an apple tree. There is a slight chill in the air so I wrap her new raspberry-pink shawl around her diminished shoulders. 'You look so pretty Mum, that colour really suits you. It even matches the flowering cherry blossom; how thoughtful of Elfie.'

'Who's Elfie?'

'Mum, Elfie's your granddaughter.'

'How old am I?'

'You're ninety-four and today's your birthday. We're having a lunch party.'

'That's too old you know darling. I don't want a party; all I want is to die.'

'Well let's get lunch over first, shall we?' I say, giving her a cuddle. 'You sit here while I fetch Aunty Dot. Aubrey will be here in a moment; there's wine and a jug of elderflower cordial. Make sure he helps himself, I shan't be a tick.'

Before long our little party is assembled and seated round a big table. The birds sing, the bees hum and the early summer blossoms nod their approval.

With everyone's glass filled, I suggest we raise them for a toast. 'To the Birthday Girl and old friends,' I say with a flourish.

'I think we should all be put down when we reach seventy,' Mum says.

Aunty Dot clings fast to her bag and showing little interest in anything else, begins to disgorge the contents onto the table. Her hair is unbrushed and she does look slightly shocking.

'Are you looking for something?' I ask. She is deaf as a post and doesn't hear me. I repeat at a shout, 'Have you lost something?' She looks up with a gummy smile, 'My teeth.'

Mother empties her glass at an alarming rate. I top it up too hastily.

'I think God's a bugger,' she says to the vicar. 'If there was a God he wouldn't let me get like this.'

I glance at Aubrey uneasily. Only three years her junior, the son of missionary and a priest to his very fingertips; a humble, self-effacing, thoroughly decent man. 'Tincture any-one?' I ask in an overly jolly manner, while trying to ignore my mother.

'I do apologise,' I say quietly to Aubrey.

Mum repeats, 'I think God's a bugger. I mean look at the state of you Dot, and look at my hands, they're all arthriticky. I can't even hold a paint brush any more . . . and I so long to paint again.'

You're managing fairly well to hold a glass, I notice.

Aubrey is too sweet to remonstrate, but a quiet aside, 'I think this attitude is not unusual in the elderly, please don't worry. I've heard it often before.'

'Mum. Please stop saying such things.'

'I'll jolly well say what I like. At my age, it's a pity if I can't.'

Short of reeling off a load of sanctimonious twaddle about all she should be grateful for, I bite my tongue and dish up the salmon mousse.

'I'm bored,' pipes up Felix. 'This is such a slow party.'

'I agree with the child,' says the Birthday Girl. 'I'm bored too.' And then, 'Doesn't Anna live up your back passage, Audrey?'

'Mum, shut up . . . and it's Aubrey!'

'Well you always say that, so why can't I?'

It's true, there has been the odd little 'in joke' about them sharing a garden, and as such, a small path to their back doors. Okay, so I admit we have had the odd cheap shot; voiced thus I blush and once again try to direct the conversation.

'Oh do look! I think that's a green woodpecker. Felix it's looking for ants. They're ground feeders, you know.'

'You're trying to change the subject. You know Audrey, Robert left me. He had an affair.'

'Please, of course Pops didn't leave you, and it's Aubrey.'

'Well if he didn't leave me, where is he then? Why isn't he here?'

'Mum! He's been dead for twenty years.'

I prefer her in la-la land. It seems so much kinder when she remembers little.

Oblivious to anything else around, Aunty Dot looks up from her travail, smiles benignly at us, and continues her rummaging. An increasing pile of detritus, fished from the nether regions of her not incommodious bag sullies my pretty table.

'Aubrey,' I ask, 'Aubrey, what's this month's charity in aid of? We thought it might be nice to make a donation on behalf of Mum. You know, to celebrate her great age.'

I choose to ignore the 'What's so great about age?' from the other side of the table. I am amused at how selective hearing can be.

'That's kind of you, it's called "Send a cow to Africa",' he says. 'It's a very worthwhile charity.'

'You know Dot, I've used the same night cream for over fifty years. It's meant to stop wrinkles. I don't think it's any good. It hasn't stopped mine,' says Mum, prodding her face with gnarled fingers.

'Well there we are, why don't we sue the maker, Mum?

It'll give you something to get your teeth into.' *Or the ones you haven't removed and left beside the pavlova. Actually, on reflection, perhaps they're the ones Aunty Dot can't find . . .*

'Make an interesting case really, I don't think they'd have bargained for a nonagenarian taking them to court,' I say, gathering up the plates and stomping off.

As I return with my lovingly prepared main course, Felix leans over and confides in me. 'That lady with the hair's just farted.'

I pretend not to hear as I dish up the chicken.

'But it's not fair,' he whines.

'What's not fair, darling?'

'If I'd done that I'd have been put on the stairs.'

We remain in silence while some of us struggle to think of something more edifying to discuss. I refill empty glasses. It is pitiful to see these once proud, elegant women reduced to this. Again I rein in unkindly thoughts. The vacillating between filial love and exasperation of such intensity alarms me. I am convinced that women, especially beautiful women, have a harder time dealing with the aging process. Their looks have been their currency and as they wane, the looks that is, they have so very little else to fall back on. Rarely do they have the resourcefulness of less attractive beings. There is so much more to despise when gazing at their reflection.

Felix sits transfixed, staring at these ancient crones. 'Great-Granma,' he pipes up. 'Will my face be all crumpled like yours when I'm older?'

'Who is this child?' Mum asks imperiously.

'He's Elfie's boy.'

'Who's Elfie?'

'The Elf's my child, you know, the one who gave you the shawl.'

'Elfie? Shawl? Who gave me this? I must give it back,' she says.

'No Mum, it was a present. You're getting a bit confused.'

'You don't know what it's like being old, you wait, one day you'll understand.'

'Are you married?' she continues. 'Robert and I never thought you would find anyone daft enough to have you. Actually, now I think about it, I couldn't stand your husband.'

I am heartened to observe, despite advanced years, there is no obvious decline in the acid tongue. After a momentary pause, a wry smile crosses my lips.

'Aubrey, you mentioned this month's charity. You don't happen to know if there's any space left on the lorry?'

Chapter 46

Apologies to a Water Hen

I have become completely captivated by some very simple little native birds. To my everlasting shame I have for years disregarded, disliked and even despised them. Based on what I now realise was an erroneous fact, I perceived them as nothing less than vermin, a predatory nuisance to the prettier and certainly gentler, and I now realise more stupid, mallard duck. I was assured in no uncertain terms that the moorhen is given to unceremoniously dragging young ducklings under the water and drowning them. So convinced that this was so, years ago I actually encouraged my father-in-law to shoot them in the mistaken belief that it was all in a good cause.

I am now not sure that is the case.

The view from the bedroom at the farm embraces a large natural pond, beyond which are some ancient oak trees, themselves the chosen habitat of a large colony of rooks, a parliament to give them their correct collective noun. This stretch of water affords me more innocent pleasure than you could imagine. It is not manicured and tweaked into some tortured feature as seen in a glossy magazine. No, there is the odd fallen tree sticking out, wonderful perches for that most elusive of birds, the kingfisher. Woodpeckers abound and I have counted at least forty mallards of various ages.

But without a doubt, the bird that has completely captivated me this year has been the humble moorhen, known locally as a water hen. While I expect I have no need to expand on its looks – they are after all fairly common – it is not very apparent which sex is which. No matter. What has utterly fascinated me is how wonderfully family-orientated they are. Nests are built by both parents in a rather random fashion among reeds or on fallen trees, high out of the water. Some country folk use this as an indication as to how wet the season will be: the higher out of the water the wetter, as it were. Oh dear. Could be that's another piece of mistaken lore. It's raining hard and I notice the latest nest floating about as I write.

These nests are a veritable amalgam of detritus. Twigs are the obvious first choice, but these industrious little birds will drag in anything that comes to beak. The nest I can spy at the moment is full of old bramble cuttings that must be seriously prickly, string, plastic bags, nettles; it seems anything goes.

Here I simply must digress to a robin's nest that was built in the porch above the front door. It was such a mess. There were bits hanging out everywhere. I was fascinated and mentioned the state of the nest to an ornithologist friend whose reply has never ceased to amuse me. It was, he suggested, built by none other than an adolescent robin; probably its first attempt and as such it was caught short, teenage pregnancies and all of that, and the result was less than perfect. But given the outcome was a success, it didn't really matter. It put me in mind of my children's bedrooms and has kept me smiling ever since.

Books tell us water hens lay between two and ten eggs; for my part I have never counted more than five. As soon as the first clutch hatches in about twenty days, the parents will start another nest somewhere else and begin all over again. And here I get to the point, the part which charms me. When these extraordinary little creatures hatch, they resemble nothing so much as tiny black pom poms on green stilts. Their feet are disproportionally huge. Unlike a waddling duck, these little chicks charge about as efficiently on land as they do in water. But best of all; while mum is off sitting on her next clutch, it falls to the elder siblings to help with the guarding and feeding of the new chicks. As a water hen can hatch up to four clutches in a season, it is not uncommon to see three different sizes of juveniles all taking care of each other.

At the moment there is a tiny chick foraging in the garden completely on its own, all the while uttering a high-pitched squeak, 'Here I am. I am here.' Every so often, mum or sibling will call back to it. If I appear, it will dive into the water and freeze under some vegetation until it sees fit to emerge. They are masterful in their attempts to hide.

I have never to this day actually seen a water hen drown a duckling. I am sure it happens; it is certainly mentioned in books. What I do know is the ratio of water hens to ducks, around here, is about one to twenty. So, if the odd duckling disappears from time to time, it's only nature and I, for one, will never try to intervene again.

Chapter 47

The Decline

Mother has had a fall and not for the first time, she is carted off to A&E in an ambulance. However, within twenty-four hours she is discharged to the local cottage hospital.

It is charming, caring and overworked; everything that Mum is not. She no longer does gracious, actually I can't quite remember if she ever did. Elegance yes, graciousness no. Her sarcasm palls around all these dear kind nurses.

'Champagne,' she retorts when the tea lady asks her what she would like to drink.

I cringe, but she giggles in a puerile way, not clever, quite simply embarrassing. I wonder if she is consciously trying to humiliate me in the way perhaps I once (albeit unwittingly) did her when I was a child.

'And what brings you back here, Mona?'

'I'm pregnant,' she says proudly.

We make a collective decision to keep her in hospital for a while. Despite nothing broken, she is frail, fragile like a little bird and there is not a lot we can do other than keep her comfortable. She is being fed regularly and monitored.

On a more delicate topic, there is a bed-wetting problem. My sister volunteers that Mum forgets to put on her 'pads'. Poor little Clarissa, her dog, who unjustly took much of the blame, died the other day, so she will no longer bear the burden of blame.

The phone rings on Tuesday. It is an exasperated matron. 'Your mother is insisting on coming home. Please can you pick her up at 2 pm?' No thought (on Mother's part) as to what we might have planned, but no matter, we go.

Three times now Mum has had a fall and been at the receiving end of the Social Services largesse. There is a lot they can provide, from zimmer frames, raising the heights of loo seats, things to facilitate bathing and anything else to enable the elderly to remain in their own home and independent for as long as possible. And both my sister and I respect Mum's greatest wish of remaining independent.

'You won't ever put me in a home,' is her constant refrain . . .

But generally, in the past, within hours of these facilitators being installed, she demands in a somewhat imperious manner that they be removed. The reasons being that they are ugly, cluttering up the house, are for old people or indeed she is much better. They are then relegated to the garage where they are collected and dispensed, we hope, to a more appreciative beneficiary.

That is until the next time Mum might be in need. And there is a next time and there will continue to be next times. At the moment we await another visit.

He is slightly late.

'So you managed to find the cottage at last?' says Mum. 'These are my two sisters.'

I hiss at her that he is a busy man. Then, to him, 'Well actually, we're her daughters.'

He smiles gently and asks if we can make a start by showing him the bathroom. It appears this and the bedroom are where things can generally unravel.

I lend Mum an arm and we lead the way.

'Now Mona, I want you to sit down on the toilet.'

'Oh do you want me to have a pee?'

'Please Mum, just go and sit down. He wants to judge the height.'

She acquiesces.

'Very good,' he says. 'Now I want you to show me what you do when you get up.'

'I wipe my bottom,' she announces.

'No, Mum,' Terry and I stifle an exasperated giggle. 'He wants to see how you actually manage to stand up.'

With this she leans forward, pulls on the wash basin and after several false starts manages to haul herself up. The basin wobbles alarmingly.

'Very good. Now what I would like to do is fit a seat with handles; this will enable you to push yourself up without pulling on the basin.' Mum feigns incomprehension.

'Just fit it – anything to make things easier,' we say in unison.

'I can't install any piece of equipment without your mother's consent.' He becomes impatient.

'Mum, do you want this?'

'I don't know.'

'It would make things easier for you. The basin will fall off soon, and then we'll be in a pickle.'

At last she agrees, the seat is fitted and her favourite chair is raised onto blocks. A commode, a Zimmer frame and two walking sticks later and the arsenal is complete.

As ever, she is less than courteous. But I trust this dear overworked man is inured to what I am beginning to think is the norm in the ancient.

Chapter 48

Compass Points

'Nick,' says Joe one morning as I am driving him to school. 'You know I want to do a foundation art course?'

'Yes darling, of course I do.'

'Well I've been thinking,' he continues, 'would you mind if I went to Exeter rather than stay about here?'

'You must do what you think best. I trust your judgement.'

'It's just that I've been talking to the Elf and she says I can stay with her and Luke. I miss them so much and it would be great to see more of them all.'

'I think it's a terrific idea; have you done anything about it though?'

'Yes,' he replies, 'and if it's okay with you, I'll go down at the end of the summer.'

While this means Joe will be leaving home sooner than expected, I am genuinely heartened by how close my children remain to each other.

*

I have often mused about what it would be like when all the children have fledged. I fondly imagined it would, at last, be my time. But now I am not so sure. I certainly hadn't bargained for being torn in three directions.

Recently I read an article about sleeping. It suggested that for the perfect night's sleep, our head should face south and our feet north, or was it east. Perhaps it was completely the other way round. Now I wish I had kept it. Could this, I wonder, be the cause of my unrest, the thrust of my problem?

At this stage, with Mum's declining health, I can only think as far as moving to Devon to lend a hand. I cannot leave it all to my dear sister. Then perhaps see where I go from there. While I know it might be the right thing, and it will be good to see more of the Elf and her burgeoning family, my heart is most definitely in Suffolk.

Mother drives me completely nuts. In fairness it is probably reciprocated. I pray daily to be more gracious with her, to be more tolerant. It doesn't always last. She is trying beyond belief, so there are times when I am in Devon that I feel I am not helping at all.

But I can't bear to think of this as a winding down. I must think of it as a new beginning.

Then I return to Bramley Cottage and think how strange it is coming back to an empty house. The place is immaculate at last; I don't necessarily dislike it, only there is a huge void.

And I'm not used to living alone. The washing machine is never full and I have to search for things to justify a wash. I stash the fridge full of goodies but there is no one to eat them. I make breadcrumbs out of unused bread and freeze them – for what? I even, dare I admit it, decant milk into little pint, plastic bottles and freeze them so that it will not be wasted! After raucous years of endless children and pandemonium, dishwashers and washing for Britain, I'm not sure I like this one bit. It all becomes rather frugal and sad.

Easter and Christmas have always been magical in this little cottage. This year I suspect none of the children will come home; they are too busy forging their own lives, which is as it should be. I hate to think they come back out of filial duty; a feeling sorry for Mum sort of thing. I want them to fly, not clip their wings. I'm not sure if I am ready to slip into old age just yet.

Then the moment I go and stay at the farm with its wide generous skies, my mood changes again. It's really wonderful to be with Jack, walking the dogs and cooking for someone once more.

So I am still completely at a loss as to know what the next move will be, but if it's to Devon, well at least I shall be surrounded by all my family. I must start thinking more positively. Yet however positively I might think, this would be a moving away from Suffolk, and drawing a line under Jack. And oh, how I would miss him, I would miss him dreadfully. The thought of a life without him saddens me more than I can say.

My compass point keeps wavering.

Chapter 49

Another Milestone

Another phone call, another drive to Devon. I arrive late on Sunday afternoon and John drives me to hospital in Exeter straight away. Mum is in the geriatric ward and looks shocking. She does recognise me, which is a great relief. However, her comments on the size of a nurse's big bottom belie my sister's theory that she is waning fast. Alarmingly, she keeps repeating that she does not want to move from here other than 'in a box then put in the ground'.

Later in the week my sister and I are invited to a meeting with the social care worker. She tells us in no uncertain terms that Mum is incapable of returning home and living on her own; as such our only option is to place her in a residential home.

We have always promised Mum that we would never do such a thing, but that was then. Now it seems we shall have to sell her beloved cottage to fund the move.

Mother's cottage nestles at the bottom of a deep valley. The hill down to it is so steep that your stomach lurches into your mouth and your ears start to pop as you approach. It is tucked away behind a high flint wall beside a ford. Twice a day a herd of black and white cows meander at their very own particular pace down the single track road, across the ford to and from their pasture.

There is an arched wooden door in the wall, which opens to reveal a pink, lime-washed, almost saccharin, quintessential Devon cottage. As you walk along a lavender-lined path, you begin to notice the peeling paint and chunks of plaster falling off the uneven walls. The thatch is sparse in places, as a result of years of birds borrowing a bit here and there.

Inside the ceilings are low, a testament to the age of the place. They knew a thing or two about building in the six-teenth century. Thick walls, tiny windows and a heavy thatch all contrive to keep it cool in the summer and warm in the winter. The sitting room is painted a deep terracotta, which serves to emphasise the smallness of the room. There is a huge inglenook fireplace complete with the original bread oven now used to hold logs.

Up a twisted winding staircase are two chaotically pro-portioned bedrooms, whose miniscule windows overlook the now neglected garden. No one minds, there is an air of genteel decay about the whole place.

The door into the garden is stiff and needs a hefty thrust to open. The path is uneven, dangerous almost, where weeds have pushed up chunks of paving. The once neat vegetable garden is completely overgrown. The trees in the orchard the grandchildren so loved to climb are gnarled and broken-limbed; it is an old, unloved garden now.

Some nights, I have lain between cool linen sheets with the heavy scent of musk roses filling the tiny bedroom and listened to the stream rippling along the ford. But there are nights when the deafening silence is punctuated by the long, low mournful bellow of a cow whose calf has been taken from her; her plaintive call clutches at my soul.

It is a charming place, infused with so many happy memories. And now my sister and I not only have to make the heartbreaking decision to sell it, but much, much worse . . . to fib to Mum.

Despite being overgrown, the garden looks so pretty; June is always a good month. Even the cats have taken to me and sit on the computer keyboard purring. We have asked the cat protection people if they could be rehomed together.

We are to tell Mum that she must have a period of convalescing before she can return to the cottage, and in the meantime pray that her mental capacity dwindles rapidly enough for her never to know that the rug has been pulled from under her. We feel wretched, despite knowing it is our only option. So the deed is done. Ironically, Mum seems wistful when we next see her, asking continually when she might be allowed home. When we explain that she is not well enough, she insists she is. It is not going to be easy. She even asks about the cats; it would be so much kinder if she knew nothing.

I spend the morning with the Elf and her children in Sidmouth, which is, under the circumstances, a wonderful change of air. We do a quick recce on a couple of care homes, which I find is depressing in the extreme. Such homes are a completely new departure for us; I had no idea how they vary. Some of the ones we visit have heavily locked front doors, and while I'm sure this is necessary, we do find it all a bit grim. I take the Elf to see the one that Terry and I have set our hearts on. Our first impression after seeing the lovely grounds is how friendly all the staff are. The front door stands open in a welcoming sort of a way and to the uninitiated it could well be a country house hotel. It appears ideal.

Last night Mum was displaying an almost normal grasp on reality, which is worrying in the extreme. This vacillating is confusing; she was so lucid Terry and I were completely thrown.

On our next hospital visit we are greeted by a nurse who tells us Mum has walked from her ward to the day room unaided. Far from delighting us, we greet this news with complete dismay. We are so confused as to how to proceed. Sell the cottage or not? The nurse takes us aside: 'Some days will be better than others,' she says, 'but basically she is declining, and living on her own is no longer an option.'

Sadly it's not that easy. Reality behoves us to continue this relentless search for a suitable home with a space for Mum. While dementia is a dreadful thing, surely it must be a blessing to slip into this phase of life not knowing too much. It is depressing beyond belief to watch Mum, frail and confused, asking when she can go home. The whole thing has been a complete learning curve for us both. The thrust of all of this really is that I am fraying at the edges.

It is going to be a nightmare. Without a doubt, the thing we find most upsetting about the whole situation is the deceit. Perhaps deceit is too strong a word, and I know it's couched in doing what is best, but it distresses us in the extreme.

This morning she is so pleased to see us and unusually sweet. She asks how the cats are. I lie. They actually went on Friday and I can't tell her.

Mum stares into the distance and agrees that she can no longer manage on her own and how helpful the nurses are. It is pitiful to see her reduced to this. I do not look forward to the next phase.

*

When my father was diagnosed with cancer he was only seventy. He asked the specialist what his course of action should be, and he replied, 'You've had your three score years and ten, I'd let nature take its course if I were you.' With various treatments he lasted another two years, then bowed out of life with the minimum of fuss. I arrived in Devon only a few days before he died. I was shocked to see how unwell Mum was; had I not known I would have thought *she* was the invalid she was so worn out. But she had insisted that Bumpa remain at home for as long as possible and nursed him single-handedly. We were left heartbroken – he was too young.

I don't know what I shall feel when Mum dies; I really don't know. What I do know is I am so glad that Bumpa isn't around to see her like this.

Chapter 50

The Fall

The French windows of Mum's new room open onto a small terrace with steps leading out to a very pretty secluded garden. The view down to Sidmouth in the distance is framed by a variety of ornamental trees. As care homes go, this was by far the nicest we could find and this room was always our first choice. But it has taken ages before the room itself has become 'available'.

One of Mum's last remaining pleasures is smoking but of course it is prohibited indoors. So Mum has had to shuffle outside for her habit. Her arthritic fingers are too weak to strike a match so she is completely dependent on one of the carers – if they have the time. So it was not only the view but the access to the great outdoors that made this room so attractive. Also it was only a few yards from where we could park a car, thus facilitating the normally frustratingly slow walk when we took her out. This was a huge advantage as her cussed independence forbade us from aiding her with either a frame or a wheelchair. 'They are for old people, darling.'

Now we could open the French windows and manoeuvre her out for a cigarette and enjoy the garden. All in all, it was a terrific move.

That was until 'the fall'.

'We've managed to get her into her chair. It's better for her to be sitting upright, we don't like them lying in their beds for too long,' the sweet nurse warns me as I turn the handle and push open the door.

The first thing I notice is the position of the bed. It has been moved and as such prevents the view that was possible when it was up against the wall. Mum is sitting in an upright chair. For reasons known only to herself she has managed to pull her trousers down. They are around her ankles, but she neither knows nor cares.

Oh Mum, I'm so relieved that you are oblivious to this phase.

Mum is asleep so I pull a chair up and sit down in front of her.

I study the frail, gaunt face while she nods away, gently unaware of my presence.

'The doctor has prescribed strong painkillers. He thinks she may have cracked some ribs. They're making her a little confused,' continues the nurse.

Mum wakes with a start. I bend forward and give her a kiss on her cheek, while trying to avoid the stubble around her mouth.

She smiles wanly, not convincing me that she actually recognises who I am.

'Hello Mum, how are you feeling?'

'Bloody awful.'

This reply is strangely reassuring.

'How are the ribs? I hear you've had another fall,' I say.

'What ribs? That thing in the corner moved.'

I stare in the direction she is pointing, at a painting of her grandmother.

'Do you mean this?' I ask.

'No, the thing beside it, it's moving.'

There is a palpable fear in her voice as I remove a large felt hat hanging beside the painting.

'This do you mean?' I say, waving it in front of her. It's too late; already she has dozed off again. I take her bony wrinkled hands in mine and try to massage them. The nails are long and claw like, reminding me of illustrations from Grimm's *Hansel and Gretel*. I make a note to bring the wherewithal to deal with them on my next visit, while pondering on symbols. What, I wonder, would you guess were I to draw long talons on scrawny fingers, a toothless grimace and a bristly chin?

Oh God, Mum, I never thought it would come to this. Always so immaculate, elegant, so careful about your appearance, and while I had no desire to emulate you, I did have a huge respect for the discipline required to constantly turn heads. But then as you explained to me, beauty is paramount to you. Always striving for perfection in everything you did. No wonder I have been such a disappointment to you sometimes. I would have understood it more were I a foundling.

She slumbers on, her mouth open and her head nodding lower with each exhalation of her feeble breath.

Now, while I do realise that you cannot simply dispose of the elderly once their quality of life diminishes, I do question the endless research into increasing longevity. Among my many friends and acquaintances, most, and I mean ninety-nine per cent, would agree that it is possible for the elderly to live too long. Mum herself spoke of this for many years.

In her more lucid moments she is not happy. She can no longer do the things that gave her pleasure: painting, collaging, gardening. She has never been a people person. As such, the idea of sitting in a communal room with other nonagenarians singing along to 'A nightingale sang in Berkeley Square', however well intentioned, appals her. Even when she lacks the ability to voice her dislike, it is there in her eyes.

The staff are charming – to a man or woman. They genuinely seem to care.

I notice her teeth lying under the bed. Having retrieved them, I give them a good scrub and hand them to her.

'Look what I've found,' I say.

Mum takes them from me, then tries to hand them back, 'Wouldn't you like them darling? Are they any use to you?'

And here we have it, other than old age, there is actually nothing wrong with her; she is quite simply frail, confused and ancient.

I really must look into living wills or the *Do not resuscitate* things that I hear mentioned. For me, I hasten to add, to facilitate matters for my children.

Harvest Time

I'm almost home after the long old drive back from the south-west. As I pass the orchard I have an idea. It is harvest and I am free for the first time in ages. I see Trevor on the forecourt so I jam on the brakes. Over the years he and his wife Sandy have become friends of mine. Not only were our children at primary school together, but there are shared interests with poultry and horses.

'Do you need any apple pickers?' I ask my man of words.

'We always need them; no one wants land work these days. Why do you ask?' he says.

'Well I've just taken Joe down to Devon, he's at art school there and I don't fancy being in an empty house at the moment,' I say. 'I was just thinking, it's years since I spent any time with the wagon. Would you mind if I brought it here and stayed in the orchard while I worked? It would be great.'

'Not in the least, that'll be fine,' he says. 'You can tether the horse by the house.'

'I'd love to if I had a horse,' I say, 'but I've pensioned Doris off now. Jack's taken her back to the farm. We've got a couple of youngsters but they're not broken to harness yet.'

'Are you saying you want me to collect it on the trailer for you?' asks Trevor.

In truth I hadn't thought about how to move it. But I smile a pleading kind of a smile, and with a 'Would you really, that would be terrific' sort of a reply, the matter is sorted.

While he may not be given to saying a great deal, Trevor more than makes up for it in matters practical. True to his word, he collects the wagon and by the time I arrive, it's unloaded and tucked up safely by a hedge. Beside it he has even thought to leave me a huge pile of freshly chopped wood.

My first chore – I say chore but it is actually a complete delight – is to get the fire going. Then I walk down to the house to fetch water. As I thump in the kettle hooks and unpack my motley collection of blackened pots and pans, I'm in my element. I fill the kettle and swing it over the now-blazing fire.

It's late afternoon and for the first time in years, with no one to please but myself, I grab a basket and set off for a leisurely stroll around the orchards. While most of the trees are the familiar Cox's Orange Pippin, they are interspersed with pollinators laden down with bright red apples. It is a fabulous sight. To one side I am delighted to see row upon row of my own personal favourite, Bramley. I pick a couple and breathe deep of the late summer air.

I feast on plump, juicy blackberries as I fill my basket. Already I can picture them mixed with cooking apples stewing gently away by the side of my fire. Beneath an ancient tree I see some mushrooms. I'm pretty certain I know what they are, but just in case, I shall verify them first. I've thought fit to bring my field guide to edible British mushrooms, so for old times' sake I'll double-check. That would make Joe smile.

As I approach the wagon with my basket full of gleanings, I'm overcome, once more, with that 'perfect moment' feeling.

I remember my father, although I cannot believe he's been dead for over twenty years, I feel he is here with me now. I know now, more than ever, I did the right thing spending his money on something as special as this. I don't want to remember him as a new roof. The wagon gives me more pleasure than anything else I possess; it never criticises or makes demands on me. It's lifted my spirit when I felt low and just to glimpse it from the cottage windows has been enough. But most importantly, it is a constant reminder to keep the dream alive.

The water in the kettle hisses away as I sit on the wagon steps and prepare a simple meal. I intend to keep cooking to a minimum and as natural as possible. With the promise of a rabbit or partridge for the pot, it looks as if mushroom omelettes are as near to hunter-gather as I am going to get.

The nights are beginning to draw in a bit early, but I am prepared. I light the storm lantern and hang it above the door. Inside the wagon there is the cosy glow of an oil lamp and I've already put a hot-water bottle in my bed knowing, as I now do, how much easier it is to be organised about such things.

Trevor and Sandy appear out of the dark, a chair in one hand and a bottle in the other. I throw more wood on the fire and we watch the flames as they dance up into the night sky while the smell of the apple wood fills the air.

Trevor goes off to check his traps, leaving Sandy and me to catch up.

'How are the children?' says Sandy. 'I haven't seen them in years. I know you told me the Elf had moved south and has a family. But what about Dan, he was such a character at school?'

'You're right – he was a bit of a handful. It's odd though, he's the one who's really surprised me, he's so hard-working, almost too much so.'

'What about your lot?' I ask, kicking a piece of log into the fire.

'Oh they're fine. Only Lucy's left home. I just wish the other two would hurry up about it,' she laughed.

'I don't believe you mean that,' I say. 'I couldn't wait for my lot to go and now they have . . . well, I don't know.'

'What about Joe?' asks Sandy. 'What's he up to?'

'Oh poor old Joe, he hit a rocky patch, but I'm sure he was just missing the other two. He gets on so well with Luke, actually we all do. I think I like him better than my own kids,' I joke.

When I first went apple picking all those years ago, it was my first bit of gainful employment since becoming a mother. Thinking back now, I have the distinct impression that I felt it was a bit beneath me. The '*Could have done better*' so familiar in my school reports would echo around my head.

The work is as relentless as it ever was. What has changed, however, is my attitude. I no longer regard it as menial, quite the reverse; I regard it as a privilege. I find there is something wonderfully meditative in such repetitive work.

It is good to be working with real people, people who lead honest, unspoilt lives. The sheer joy of being out of doors with nature makes me delight in the elements and I love feeling physically exhausted at the end of a day.

Harvesting apples is glorious. September can be a beautiful month: crisp mornings and the last of the summer sun. Is it universal, or simply me; the moment something becomes finite, I savour it more deeply?

If time is the only currency we are all dealt in equal amounts, I try to quantify why it passes or appears to pass so much more quickly with age. I wonder if it has anything to do with our restless minds. I know I should live in the now – children do. Rather than think of all the undone things in my life and the frenetic mad labour I've imposed on myself, perhaps if I simply sat down by a hedge with a book or attempted to identify butterflies, perhaps time would then pass as slowly as it once did.

There is a feeling in a Mary Newcomb painting or Ronald Blythe essay that their time passes more slowly, more rhythmically. There's no doubt, dealing with an ancient mother constantly reminds me of my own mortality.

I am struck by how deserted the countryside appears. There is even a paucity of wildlife; a solitary swallow swoops over the stubble, the ubiquitous rabbit grazes on the margin, but so very little else.

The fields are cut. Well mostly. I struggle to articulate what I feel at such times: the end of the year's work, the heralding of autumn and the beginning of a new cycle. In the Pied Piper of Hamelin, when he has led all the children into the hills, a silence falls about the town. Only it's computers, machinery and the pace of life that seems to isolate us now. Rarely do you see children biking or playing in the lanes. Yes, there are middle-aged joggers and dedicated cyclists in ridiculous clothes, but seldom youngsters simply 'being'.

I remember a conversation I had with Terry. It was on a soulful morning such as this.

'I've got it!' I said. 'St George wasn't killing a real dragon . . . the dragon simply represents Evil!'

'What did you just say?' she asked.

'I said I think it wasn't really about a dragon, it was just about good overcoming bad. What do you think?'

'I'll tell you exactly what I think. I think you think too much rubbish. I'm thinking how many potatoes to peel for supper tonight and what vegetables would be nice with lamb.'

Dear, shy Trevor is still a man of few words. That elusive trait, the one I find so endearing in people, I now think to define as a contentment; an ease with their lot, an acceptance, a feeling happy in their skin. I find it an irresistible quality.

Mum used often to say *More is less*. I think perhaps now I'm beginning to understand what she means.

Loneliness is the sadness of being alone. Solitude is the joy of being alone.

It's heaven here, alone in the orchard with the wagon. I've made up my mind – I shall buy another wagon horse and take off in it next spring. The children were never too keen on it, always belly-aching about missing a sleepover or some drivel on the telly. But I don't have to worry about that now. I can, I shall, do it before it's too late. And yet I am still so torn between Bramley Cottage and Devon; to stay or go. Then there is Jack and the farm. Perhaps I should try to resolve that dilemma before I take to the open road.

I wonder if it's time to let the cottage go, to sell it. It would certainly free me up to follow my dreams. And I would still have all the marvellous memories. We will always have those.

Chapter 51

Osmosis

I am of the opinion that the only way I have learnt in life is by making my own mistakes. With the knowledge that I've made enough of those, I do think it has been a great deal more effective than any amount of unsolicited advice, well-intentioned or otherwise.

I know I have erred on the side of caution when counselling my own children, preferring instead to trust that with the right set of values, they too will find their own path. I admit there have been moments when I wondered if my parenting skills were a tad dilatory; I know others questioned it.

But I'm infused with a warm glow of maternal pride as I sit at a huge table in the Elf's chaotic kitchen preparing for Easter with my grandchildren. Well, two of them actually, Billie and Tobi. I note with interest that Felix is already given to spending more of his time on the stairs for being mischievous than he does in the body of the family.

'Does Felix remind you of anyone, Mother dearest?' says Dan, winking at me. He's at the other end of the table helping Tobi model tiny little Easter chicks out of Fimo.

The morning started well; there was something wonderfully reassuring getting out of bed and stubbing my toe on a Lego spaceship. That Billie's pet mice had kept me awake half the night whirring about on their wheel was small matter compared to the magnanimity of my granddaughter giving up her bedroom for my visit.

'Why is Felix on the stairs again? Poor little sprout, it's Easter Day. Darling, do let him join us,' I say to the Elf.

She's stirring a pan of lemon curd, while Billie, who's dressed as a fairy, stands on a chair beside her watching intently. With her long flaxen hair and bare legs, she is the image of her mother when she was a child.

'Okay – tell him he can come and join us. But I warn you Dan, don't start egging him on.'

'Hi Felix, come and sit beside us,' says Dan, patting a chair. 'Look, here's a bit of clay. See if you can model it into something nice for Granny Nit.'

'Why are you called Granny Nit?' Felix asks, rolling his piece of Fimo up and down the table. 'Have you got nits? I've got them, haven't I, Mum?'

'No, you have not,' says Elfie emphatically.

'I have,' says Felix, raising his voice and scratching his head. 'You were looking for them the other night. You said you were!'

'I was looking to see if you might have some and you haven't . . . oh forget it.'

'I started saying Granny Nit because I got muddled with Nick,' explains Billie from her vantage point above the stove.

'Tobi, will you and Billie set the table while I go and hide the eggs,' says the Elf. 'Come on Nick, you can help me.'

We go into the garden where Luke is putting the finishing touches to a treehouse for the children; Joe is lending him a hand.

As I wander about popping little brightly coloured eggs into every obscure crevice I can find, I hear my mother's words echo around my head. *Be careful to leave a little something for yourself once the children are grown.*

I once wrote that the only thing I feared in life was waking up and realising it was all too late, although I'm not quite sure I knew what I meant. But it's just dawned on me – perhaps now is the time for me to follow my dreams once more.

And the most wonderful thing is, as all the children appear so at ease with their lot, so confident on their chosen paths, I know they will not only approve but positively applaud my decision.

'Granny Nit,' says Felix, coming into the garden and taking my hand, 'Dan says you were really naughty when you were little. Were you, what did you do?'

'One of these days, darling, when you're a little older, I'll tell you.'

Chapter 53

Moving On

While we knew it would not be easy selling Mum's cottage and unravelling her life, fortunately my sister and I were never at variance as to which of her belongings to keep. Possessions that would not only resonate with her, but would positively enrich this new phase in a nursing home; curtailing her life as we knew we must.

Apart from the more obvious choices of family portraits and photographs to line the institutionalised walls, the sculptures she so loved and a few of the great-grandchildren's offerings, there were two immutables: her easel and a fine looking-glass.

Now we wonder if we've been overly optimistic cluttering such a small space with a full-sized easel when she purports to lack the will or ability to ever paint again.

I approach her room with the usual trepidation, wondering what more I can possibly find to convince me old age is not for the faint-hearted.

I no longer knock, for fear of waking her. Instead I push open the door, but the bed is empty.

Mum is standing at her easel, as straight as her frail body will allow. In her left hand she clasps her cane but in the other is a paint brush. She doesn't see me at first, so intent is she on daubing great splashes of colour onto her beloved canvas.

I stand in the doorway and watch. This is the mother I love, this is the mother I want to hold onto forever.

Her easel faces the garden. As I move closer I can see she is capturing a tree in the far distance. And in the foreground there is the merest outline of a tall, elegant figure looking out towards it.

She senses my presence and turns. 'Oh darling. How wonderful to see you, give me a hug,' she says. 'I do love you, you know.'

I wrap my arms about her diminished frame and hold her tight. 'I love you too, Mum.'

'Isn't it funny,' she continues, 'I'm shrinking. You used to look up to me.'

While I consulted the children as to the sale of Bramley Cottage, I was mindful that it was my decision and no one else's; although matters pecuniary did play their part. I am not in a position to run a house while spending great swathes of time at the other end of the country.

I know I have made the right decision but there is so very much I shall miss.

As the removal men set to work, I go for one last soulful walk around the village. I see so many of the cottages that once teemed with life are now silent; so many of the dear characters who so enriched our lives, now gone. It feels as if the heart has drained out of the village, just like the heart has drained out of our cottage.

I meander along the narrow coastal path as it wends its

way through ancient heathland. An adder basking in the late afternoon sun slithers silently into the purple heather. There is a sheer drop of some fifty feet to my right as I draw near the last remaining gravestone. It sits precariously, perched at the very edge, patiently awaiting its fate when the next chunk of cliff is undermined by the crashing waves below.

Above me skylarks trill in the near-perfect sky, while way beneath, sand martins dart to and from their burrows in the red sandy cliffs. In the far distance, out beyond the rich mosaic of vegetation, over the grazing marshes, I catch a last glimpse of the lighthouse as it flashes across the bay.

I study the view and as if by magic, a sea fret rolls in, cowling everywhere with its ghostly mist.

As I reach the cottage, my eyes gradually adjust to the haze. I walk in through the front door as I once did all those years ago. With all our belongings gone, there are only memories now.

The red light that has glowed constantly in the hall, warming our darkest moments, is switched off. But I can still hear children's laughter, everywhere, echoing through the empty rooms. Upstairs in the corridor there's a little tousled-haired chap with his nose in a nature book, while his sister skips past dressed as a fairy, sprinkling us once more with her magic dust. I hear my mother's words mingle with the laughter: *'Without a husband to pander to you are free to do as you like.'*

In the kitchen the children and I feast once more on lobsters and samphire. I hear the clinking of glasses as we raise them in a toast to the countless happy memories. The cottage vibrates with life again and I question my decision.

At the bottom of the garden beneath the old cedar tree, Dan stares out towards the sea. I walk down and put my arm around his shoulder – he is my little boy again. We remain in our own silent worlds, too choked to say a word.

Then as quickly as the fret came, it goes. As the magic dissipates, I know it's time for me to leave.

I used to say I disliked choice. Now I'm almost in a position to plough my own furrow, dividing my time between Jack's farm in Suffolk and my family in Devon. I know how lucky I am.

I bend down and pick up the red light bulb that lies discarded on the floor. Who knows when I might need it again?

So it's with a full heart that I close the door and turn the key for the last time.

I can hear Jack sounding the car horn. Perhaps there are others in need of my conjuring skills.

It's my turn now! Grasp it!

Acknowledgements

Without wishing to run on, there are many people who I would like to thank for their encouragement and support:

most importantly, a massive thank you to all my family, including Jack, for being such terrific sports;

thank you also to Alan Titchmarsh, the whole team at *The Alan Titchmarsh Show* and everyone who was involved in the People's Author Competition, particularly Amanda Harris, Luigi Bonomi and Gervase Phinn, for giving me this amazing opportunity;

thanks to Susanna Abbott and everyone at Orion for turning the book into a reality;

to Ruby Ormerod, my mentor, for all her sound advice and, in particular, my heartfelt thanks to Kate Cheasman for persuading me to have a go;

lastly, thank you so very much to my terrific editor Celia Hayley for her tireless effort in coaxing me into finishing the manuscript. Not an easy task.